The Turn of the Tide

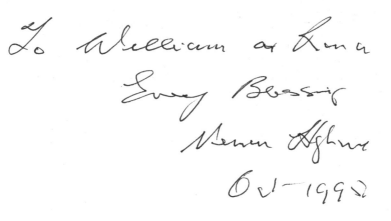

THE TURN
OF
THE TIDE

When God Floods His Church
with True Revival Blessing

By

W. Vernon Higham

With Foreword By
Richard Owen Roberts

Published Jointly by
The Heath Trust, Cardiff, Wales
and
International Awakening Press
Wheaton, Illinois
1995

Published By
INTERNATIONAL AWAKENING PRESS
P. O. Box 232
Wheaton, Illinois 60189 U.S.A.
A Division Of
International Awakening Ministries, Inc.
and
THE HEATH TRUST
31 Whitechurch Road
Cardiff, South Wales CF4 3JN

Printed in the United States of America

ISBN 0-926474-15-4

Library of Congress
Catalogue Card Numbers 95-078315

All Scripture references are from the
King James Version of the Bible.

ACKNOWLEDGEMENT

This book is based on a series of expository addresses on the subject of Revival that were preached by the author at the Evangelical Movement of Wales Annual Conference held at Aberystwyth, West Wales, on August 13-18, 1984.

Recordings of the original addresses are available on tape from the Evangelical Movement of Wales at Bryntirion House, Bridgend, South Wales, and in tape album form from the Heath Christian Bookshop, 31 Whitchurch Road, Cardiff, South Wales.

All hymns are by the author unless otherwise identified.

CONTENTS

FOREWORD

Will the "land of revivals" ever experience revival again?

Whereas powerful revivals occurred with wonderful frequency in Wales—perhaps on average every twenty to thirty years—from the early Puritan period until the end of the nineteenth century, it has been a long, dry season since the revival of 1904-1905. Has it been so long and is the moral and spiritual declension so great that even God Himself cannot turn things back? Indeed, are we, as some leaders confidently affirm, living in a post-Christian age?

As the Church has approached the end of its twentieth century, it has been increasingly common to hear the clamoring voices of self-appointed prophets declaring that the days of revival are forever past. Among them are those who have gone so far as to predict that the next event on God's calendar is the end. Some among them appear to believe that things have never been so bad before and that they can do nothing, at this late date in human history, but get worse and worse. Are they right? Are things worse now than ever before? Not if history speaks truthfully! Does deep moral and spiritual declension indicate the nearness of the end? Dozens of times in the past it has indicated something very different, very hopeful, very exciting! Every great revival of the past has been preceded by a terrible moral and spiritual decline. Are there not greater reasons to believe that the deplorable conditions of this age are precursors of splendid divine blessings than to suppose that things can only grow worse and worse until finally the end comes?

Others in the Church seem to like things the way they are so well that the last thing in the world they would want would be a moral and spiritual upheaval that would restore righteousness to the land and so thoroughly reveal the utter wickedness of all sin that they would be forced either to repent and turn from their evil ways or to practice their filthy deeds under the cover of darkness or behind closed doors. They would rather see the whole world in hell, themselves included, than see a restoration of that spirit of holiness that would make their vile living as acceptable in society as furtive cockroaches on the dining room table.

Still other professing Christians appear so busy about their religious lives and endless schemes of "good works" that they seem not yet to have noticed God's absence from the Church and from the land. Whether or not revival can happen again or will happen again is apparently a matter of supreme indifference to them.

Revival, however, is neither impossible, undesirable, nor unimportant to a growing number of prudent believers throughout the principality. They live with the conviction that an unchanging God is still upon His throne. They believe that a time of almost insane lawlessness and licentiousness is the very time God may be expected to once again violently enter the stream of human history. They know that God delights to surprise the indifferent and to overpower the self-righteous. In short, they are convinced that the time is ripe for revival, and they are busy making ready their hearts for the awakening to come.

Vernon Higham is among this band of loyal stalwarts who have neither bowed their knees to Baal nor stiffened their necks against the God who inhabits eternity. He believes revival is needed. He believes revival can be expected. He believes God still delights to meet His people at the point of their felt need.

Using Isaiah sixty-two as a base, Pastor Higham of the Heath Church, Cardiff, begins this precious volume by exploring, in fresh and flavorful language, this tremendous need of revival. He carefully demonstrates that the fact of the tide having been out for a long time does not prove that it will never return again but rather that those who have erected their tents of pleasure on the tidal flats are in for a thorough soaking.

From Isaiah sixty-three, Pastor Higham portrays the appropriate heart cry for God which is the heart cry of revival in seasons of declension. By sagaciously interweaving pungent anecdotes from revival history with the biblical text, the author sharpens our hearts' longings and quickens our cries for God to do it again and to do it quickly.

A third chapter focuses on the burden for revival and is based on the first seven verses of Isaiah sixty-four. As is true throughout the volume, Pastor Higham skillfully interweaves quotations from hymns, both common and uncommon, with his revival anecdotes and textual development. Striking indeed is the brief statement concerning "singing in the air" which was a not uncommon phenomena of past movements of the Holy Spirit in Wales.

The final chapter (Isaiah 64:8-12) is intended to quicken our hope for revival. Indeed, a reader would have to have a tragically hardened heart not to experience something of a true quickening in reading this section.

It is my deep conviction that the life of an author is as important as his printed words. A man can write well but undermine his words by his life. A man may even write poorly and yet live in such a way as to make his message powerful. Vernon Higham, by God's grace, has done both. He has written well, and he has backed up his writing with a life lived for the glory of God. His long, faithful years of ministry at Heath Evangelical Church in Cardiff are well known. His love of Christ and commitment to Holy Scripture are clearly proven to be a vital part of who he is. The devotion of his wife and children are yet an added testimony to the validity of this book.

THE TURN OF THE TIDE

It is with great pleasure that I commend it to readers everywhere. While Pastor Higham is a Welshman and speaks very effectively to the Welsh scene, the book is in no sense provincial. Its precious truths have power to enlighten, to stir, to challenge, to convict, to encourage, and to inspire the hearts of men and women the wide world over.

As you read it, let the obvious need of revival stir your heart to deep, deep longings for God Himself. Let your growing burden for revival be saturated with the hope that the unchanging God will revive His people once again.

Richard Owen Roberts
Wheaton, Illinois, USA

PREFACE

Revivals can be neither manufactured nor initiated; they are God-given. It could, of course, be said, "If they are such, can we not therefore leave this matter of revival in His hands hoping vaguely that maybe in this coming generation, or the next, mercy will be shown towards us?" But this is not how we understand the nature or the method of God's dealings with His people, for in the Bible we find men and women who knew all the while that nothing could happen without God's blessing, yet who still ventured to plead and argue and strive with God in prayer until that time when His favor was at long last granted to them.

How does this picture square up with our own experiences in this present day and age? Is it not true, and should we not now be admitting the fact that, as God's Church, we have become in this generation desperately weak and tragically ineffective? As God's people, is it not true that we really have become as nothing in the sight of society, that our voice counts for nothing, and that it seems in many ways as if we are a forsaken people? Is it not also a fact that we can continue in our little evangelical chapels, blissfully unaware of the need, unless He opens our eyes?

When reading books on revival, I am always struck by the first few chapters: those chapters that deal, as it were, with the preparation and groundwork preceding the blessing itself. The time span involved in the preparation can cover ten, twenty, even thirty years; all this time contrasting sharply with the period of refreshing and uplifting itself, which may be over in less than a year. What priceless lessons are those that are always included in these opening chapters! What an intimate story it would be if fully unfolded! What depth of experiences proven and recorded, what anguish of spirit, what a stirring in the hearts and souls of men!

I trust and believe that it is not impossible for us today to be venturing through such opening chapters. It may be that we have a few more pages to go before we reach the desired place, but we should not be discouraged. Even along the way, the lessons taught are both invaluable in themselves as well as being needed in order to guide us and finally bring us into those times of true revival. Sometimes it takes us many years to learn one small lesson, but when we learn that lesson, how precious a thing it is and what a beautiful view it gives us of God! He may take us on many a winding journey and through many a troubled water, but it is in this way that we learn more of the greatness and glory of our God.

W. Vernon Higham
July 1995

Chapter 1

THE NEED FOR REVIVAL
(Isaiah 62)

How can we describe this great prophet Isaiah? His book is frequently referred to as "the Gospel in the Old Testament." Here is a man who often expresses deep anguish as he writes of the burden upon his heart. Here is a man who cares. Do we care? Are we willing to see this terrible spiritual declension continue and the evangelical faith derided as if it were some freakish little sect that man can jibe at? Are we willing that men should preach the Gospel lightly and make it a thing of entertainment? Are we willing that the glorious Gospel of our gracious God should be treated in any way other than with deep reverence? Should we not always remember with whom we are dealing—that we are, in fact, dealing with the one and only Almighty and Holy God?

The Gospel message itself is both joyous and glorious. It announces and includes a tremendous and happy end for our immortal souls. Yet, all the while, the preaching of this Gospel is still a great and serious matter in this silly, flippant, happy-go-lucky little age with its deep, deep sorrows and its profound problems. Its superficial gaiety is by no means an indication of the terrible and very real mess it is in.

Why it is, in view of these things, that we in the Church so often try to imitate the world's superficiality is beyond my understanding. We are the Lord's people. Our directive and mandate is from above. Therefore, there is no call or need for us to borrow worldly ways and attitudes. We are faced with a formidable host opposing the Christian Gospel while the ranks of the faithful are in disarray.

In order to convey further something of what I mean, allow me to use an illustration given by an old Welsh preacher. Imagine a beautiful beach washed regularly by the tide, cleansing, purifying, and removing from it all that is unclean. Let the land covered by the beach be described, if you like, as God's acres. One day, however, the tide happens to go out further than usual, and soon the people begin to say that the tide will never come in again; that there will never be, in God's acres, a restoration of the preached Word of God; that people will never again tolerate sitting in uncomfortable pews for hours nor be willing to subject themselves to the ministry of a pastor; that the giving of a whole day to the worship of God is surely become a thing of the past. The tide has gone right out, and it seems as if there is no God in existence at all.

A kind of boldness then appears, and we see in our illustration temporary buildings of every conceivable kind erected on the beach. Many of them are there for pleasure. The invading crowd that has come to occupy the buildings is shouting that man must be made happy. Much time and energy is spent making people laugh and feel comfortable in the delusion that all is well. People can go from one pleasure tent to another and be amused and seemingly satisfied for a time. Temporary happiness is offered and temporary happiness is obtained. There are, in fact, even religious tents on the beach, each giving platform to various teachings. New and strange voices are heard. Some are mixed in with an evangelical type of jargon, others with none. In and among these religious tents we also find the cults. One can hardly wend their way between the tents or avoid the din of the slick salesmen loudly recommending their wares and offering their various packages, crying: "Here you will be happy with our formula, our notion, and our way!" And so babble a multitude of voices from myriad tents. Some of the salesmen are very, very bold indeed. They will even pitch their tents on the water's edge and dare the very waves. This is especially true of those who have erected their tents of error within the bounds of what is agreed by all to be the accepted historic Christianity. False prophets and humanists alike all shout together in unison, "He is not coming back. We shall never be corrected. We are the true masters of our time and destiny."

This is the kind of age we live in, and if anybody, anywhere, should dare to suggest that some day the tide might turn and come in, men would probably reply, "The tide come in? How can it come in when there isn't any room for the water? Come in? It can't come in! We won't let it come in! This is our beach! It no longer belongs to Him!" And so it is that we come to realize that there seems to be so very little room in our lives for God.

We could bury ourselves in the statistics which tell of the decline in the various traditional religious denominations, of the tiny numbers of God's people and, if such figures were available, how very few even of them would have a real burden or concern for the deeper things of God. Ichabod—"The glory is departed"—is written large whichever way we turn.

One particular incident stays in my memory. Years ago, preaching in a very beautiful chapel in North Wales, when still a theological student, I remember thinking to myself, "When I become a minister I would very much want to have a chapel like this." The people were lovely people. The chapel was very impressive. There were plenty of buildings at the rear and so there were no problems for the future. Indeed, it seemed ideal for a young minister, and although they were not considering me, I was simply musing how lovely a chapel it was. Years later, I happened to be travelling through that part of the country and stopped for petrol. Then I looked and saw what I really didn't want to see at all. The facade of the building was gone—it had become a petrol station. Above, I could see the name of the chapel. Inside, there were no pews, and between the galleries was suspended a double decker bus. I could not believe it—it was like an arrow to my heart! Oh, I knew some chapels had become bingo halls and all sorts of uses had been made of them, but this was different again somehow. The blow was far greater than usual. For the first few seconds I did no more than view what is today a very common sight; then suddenly the full force of the tragedy dawned upon me. I realized that there was no prayer, no preaching, no congregation—only the noise of hammer and machinery, shouting and swearing, in a place where once men waited on God and preached the unsearchable riches of Christ. This brought it all home to me—the great need, not only of my own land, the islands of Britain, but also that of the whole world.

Think for a moment of the place where you have been fortunate enough perhaps to be given work and employment. You are blessed indeed if there is another Christian believer in that work place. Usually you are the only one. It is but a reflection of the terrible decline and proof of the fact that the mass of people in our present society, in their dealings or lack of dealings with God, do not stop to give Him even the least thought. Even the larger, "successful," evangelical congregations of the land are still insignificant and are as a nothing compared with the myriad multitudes and milling masses which still remain on the beach of our illustration.

Yet, more importantly, how then can we be inspired to believe that God can visit His people? Let us not be solely preoccupied with the multitudes outside. Our hearts are burdened for them but let us now be concerned also for the message that God may have for us. A.W. Tozer wrote many excellent books with titles almost as good as their contents! One such book bears the title, *God Tells the Man who Cares.* Again we can ask the question, "Do we care?" Do you care—really care—care enough to support the things of God in every way you possibly can? Will you support your pastor? Will you support your elders and deacons? Will you encourage your fellow members, help with the Sunday school, and do what you can in every avenue of the work of the church? Are you willing to care on that level? In Isaiah sixty-two, verse six, for example, we learn very definitely that God is a God who cares.

> I have set watchmen upon thy walls, O Jerusalem, which shall never hold their peace day nor night: ye that make mention of the Lord, keep not silence.

Wonderful, caring words, are they not? We all know, when we think of a medium like television or radio, that although there are religious services and the occasional evangelical one, the mass of the material that is produced has nothing at all to do with God. In some respects the night is far spent. When we consider these things, it makes us feel so very feeble regarding the enormous task that confronts us in this age. Still we ask ourselves the question, "Do we care?"

It may be that something has taken the edge off our spiritual sense of reality. We can learn our doctrines and delight in them but, because of the ease of the age, we learn them so very comfortably. We can even have wonderful spiritual experiences and spend much time telling others about them, rather than getting on with the things of God in the light of those experiences. We ourselves seem to be drunk with the idea that people must be entertained and be made happy rather than pursuing the great task that God has put before us. One missionary in our church recently made what I believe to be a very telling observation. After she had been away for four or five years, I asked her if she had noticed any difference between five years ago and now. "Yes," she answered, "there is one difference I can't help noticing. It is so apparent to me that you deny yourselves nothing." Think, Christian brother or sister, upon the thrust of her observation. Ask yourself, "Have I denied myself anything recently?" We give, but sadly we give only what we can spare. Is it not true of us all? It is only when we begin to see our own shortcomings, our selfishness, our

apathy, and our neglect, that we begin to see how far we have
to go before we can fully understand and appreciate the burden
and self-sacrificing zeal for God that is presented to us in the
life of such a man as the prophet Isaiah.

In Isaiah sixty-two, the declaration of Isaiah's vision is
outlined in the first five verses where God speaks with great
confidence through the prophet. In these verses He maintains
that He does not desire His Church to be forsaken. He does not
wish her to be a disgrace here on earth. This has never been
His desire for Zion, city of His own chosen people. These
verses will help us to consider what God really does desire and
what He would have for His Church in our own present day
and age. It is not merely the filling of buildings that is important, although obviously an empty place of worship is hardly
encouraging, and so we are in one respect, unashamedly
concerned with numbers. Don't misunderstand me. If I were
told that one person had been saved, I would of course be glad,
very glad, but if then I were told that a million people had been
swept into the Kingdom, I would be more than glad—I would
be delighted, and thrilled beyond measure. What we have is a
healthy concern always for the individual phenomenon, but its
repetition tenfold or a hundredfold would be even more wel-
come. We are grateful for the day of small things, but oh, that
God would soon bring us days filled with the greater! This is
what we yearn for without any ingratitude in any respect
whatsoever for the ones and twos who are saved here and there,
even in the midst of this perverse and untoward generation.

How does our burden compare then with that of Isaiah?
Consider again that very first verse:

> For Zion's sake will I not hold my peace, and for
> Jerusalem's sake I will not rest, until the righteousness
> thereof go forth as brightness, and the salvation thereof
> as a lamp that burneth.

What we have here is the prophet resting on God's covenant promise and resolving that He will not keep silent until he sees that Zion is indeed made righteous, and that she in truth does shine brightly in such a way that tells all who view her of the salvation that she has found in God.

Let me bring in another illustration. Think of a pleasant winter's night. There is your chapel in the distance, perhaps on a hill. People are wending their way in the direction of the building; lamps can be seen shining through the windows. Think now how much more wonderful it would be if, as we also made our way towards the meeting, we knew that the church had become filled with people reflecting the brightness of His glory and giving undeniable proof that the light of His salvation was indeed burning in their hearts as also in all the other congregations throughout the land. This is the wonderful picture that the prophet places here in the passage. His petition—notice how he persists regarding it—is for the story and knowledge of salvation to go forth as a burning light, coupled with the determination that the Gospel of God should and must succeed in reaching and completing its work in the hearts of men. Just think of the transformation that is here promised in the second verse:

> And the Gentiles shall see thy righteousness, and all kings thy glory: and thou shalt be called by a new name, which the mouth of the Lord shall name.

The address, as we have suggested already, is to a church that is by all appearances deserted and forsaken. In this direction, there are maybe a handful of people, only half believing; in that direction, a few evangelicals who only half pray. God is looking in this or that direction towards His Church on earth, and He desires a time when "the Gentiles shall see thy righteousness, and all kings thy glory. . . ." Imagine the astonishment that would follow were scriptural revival to occur again in our generation on a global scale. Perhaps a declaration would be made before the United Nations, reading as follows—"Something has happened in the Church of God. God is in the midst of His people, mighty to save! France has fallen into the arms of God! Russia has fallen! Britain has fallen in the war of the Lamb! The United States has succumbed!" The United Nations would, I am sure, find it strange to have to begin to deal with nations now so different and changed in calibre. New representatives would probably have to be appointed. New principles would be sought after and established. More importantly, the Church would once again be the talking point among the Gentiles. Is it possible? Of course it is! Believe it! Our Almighty God is mighty enough to perform all that we have here described. Lift up your heart! Lift up, open, and enlarge your mind and imagination! Forget the puny little god that we put in the corner of a shelf on a Sunday! Open your eyes to see Him—Omnipotent, Omnipresent, Omniscient, Everlasting, Almighty, and Glorious God!

It is this God that looks at His Church and says in verse three:

Thou shalt also be a crown of glory in the hand of the
Lord, and a royal diadem in the hand of thy God.

He who could, if He wanted, gather before Himself the whole multitude of nations, here chooses to describe rather the beauty of the Church of God on earth and His purposes for her. She is His pride. His love is unending toward her. Have we grasped these truths and realized how important they are in our present situation? How clear is your vision of the immensity and holiness of God? Can you hear the Church in her response to the promised blessing? "I am not ready. I cannot fathom it. It hurts too much to think about it. I do not feel myself to be a royal diadem or a crown of glory. I am Thy Church, but look at me! By heresies torn, by schisms oppressed, by apathy hampered and stifled!"

Then with loving kindness He declares:

> Thou shalt no more be termed Forsaken; neither shall
> thy land any more be termed Desolate (verse 4a).

How appropriate these illustrations are. If somebody should look at our land today and then enquire about the condition of the Church of God, after taking a good long view, their considered answer would almost certainly have to be: "She is desolate! She is as if forsaken! Yet she remains God's Church, and so the promise stands; a bright future still lies before her despite all signs to the contrary."

> But thou shalt be called Hephzibah, and thy land
> Beulah: for the Lord delighteth in thee, and thy land
> shall be married (verse 4b).

Imagine it! No more forsaken but rather a Church married to her God!

> For as a young man marrieth a virgin, so shall thy sons
> marry thee: and as the bridegroom rejoiceth over the
> bride, so shall thy God rejoice over thee (verse 5).

The Church will give birth to many sons as the bride of the Lord, and God shall rejoice in His inheritance. That which was once forsaken, is now beloved.

Where then do we begin? Where does God begin? Can God do something new yet again, even with this present generation? People are no different; our sins are the same. Do we believe in the sovereignty of God? I am sure we do, but do we understand His sovereignty? Or do we rather misunderstand it deliberately, misusing it in order to shun our responsibility and excuse our neglect? I well remember that Dr. Martyn Lloyd-Jones used to remind us frequently, "God is sovereign, but remember that He is a sovereign, active God, working out His purposes in the midst of His people."

Let us consider once again the solemn words of positive responsibility in verse six:

> I have set watchmen upon thy walls, O Jerusalem, which shall never hold their peace day nor night: ye that make mention of the Lord, keep not silence.

This is the first thing that this active God will do—He will settle this matter of the watchmen. These watchmen not only represent the prophets of the Old Testament, but they also, of course, represent the faithful ministers of the New Testament and of the Gospel. Remember this truth whoever you are and whatever your age—in particular, every new young generation of Christians should always seek to remember that a person who is called to serve the Lord Jesus Christ in the ministry is the Lord's anointed. His is a high office, a fearful calling, involving great responsibility. He has been given a great privilege and a very honored position. One of God's greatest gifts to His Church is a faithful minister. Oh, that God might raise up in this generation an army of God-called, God-sent, faithful ministers of the Word! Isaiah describes this office in the first three verses of chapter sixty-one. How sublime, yet how sobering for all those who have found themselves in such a position!

> The Spirit of the Lord God is upon me; because the Lord hath anointed me to preach good tidings unto the meek; He hath sent me to bind up the brokenhearted, to proclaim liberty to the captives, and the opening of the prison to them that are bound; To proclaim the acceptable year of the Lord, and the day of vengeance of our

God; to comfort all that mourn; To appoint unto them that mourn in Zion, to give unto them beauty for ashes, the oil of joy for mourning, the garment of praise for the spirit of heaviness; that they might be called trees of righteousness, the planting of the Lord, that He might be glorified.

God sets His watchmen on the walls and His messengers in the pulpits. But what will they preach? They will preach good tidings, the Gospel of our Lord and Saviour Jesus Christ. They will declare that Jesus Christ is the only begotten Son of God. They will proclaim His absolute deity and His perfect humanity. They will tell all that He lived a perfect life on this earth, and that in His death He paid the penalty for our sin. Indeed, they will insist that our sins were imputed to Him and that by faith His righteousness becomes ours. They will also proclaim that the total cost involved found its sufficiency solely in the precious blood of our Lord and Saviour Jesus Christ. They will teach that the intensity of His suffering was the intensity of all the suffering of Hell—a depth of suffering that cannot be expressed in words other than those with which He cried out on the cross: "My God, my God, why hast thou forsaken me?" Here is a degree of desolation that ensures that those who were far away from Him are now indeed effectively brought nigh unto God. This is the heart of true preaching, a preaching not only of the cross but also of the meaning of the cross, the actual doctrine of substitution, a saving work done in our stead in the realest possible sense. He died that we might live!

All too often what we hear is a preaching around the cross, but we must preach the very heart of it; it is our binding duty. We must preach this message first and foremost and then, in the light of it, we can begin to comfort those who mourn, whether it be for sin or because of the sorrows of this life. We are also commanded to try to protect the flock from the errors which abound at all times, but never more so than in this day.

Is not this our experience far too often—a new idea comes to town and the minister's heart sinks because sadly it is predictable that the crowd will run after it as they have run and sought after all the other new ideas which have gone before? Success is sweet to begin with. Then havoc is wrought and they tire of it. Another idea comes and then another, and the people are blown about by every wind of doctrine. Indeed, they will indulge in all sorts of foolish behavior, they will pursue all the latest fashionable quirks and give ear to all the trendy voices. They will do all this before and in place of recognizing and respecting God's preacher and God's Word. How tragic, how silly, how immature this behavior is; how ironic, when we remember that it is here alone, in this neglected ordinance of the preaching of God's Word, that we are promised and provided with the only real and true means of discovering the unsearchable riches of Christ and so, also, the forgiveness of sins which He alone can give! It is here that we find peace with God and acceptance in the sight of the Almighty which leads "to an inheritance incorruptible, and undefiled, and that fadeth not away, reserved in heaven" (I Peter 1:4). It is then that our souls are satisfied and our hopes met. In that moment we are given "beauty for ashes, the oil of joy for mourning, and the garment of praise for the spirit of heaviness" (Isaiah 61:3).

Should not the preachers of the Word arise then and speak, preach, plead, and pray for this Gospel? You may say, "We do it already." Or you may say, "We will do it." I say, "We must do it!" We must do it clearly and in the power of the Spirit, for sadly there is a great dearth of these preachers. But listen again. God says He wants something more even than preaching: He wants us first and foremost to learn to pray. What sort of prayer is He looking for? It is described as follows:

And give Him no rest, till He establish, and till He make Jerusalem a praise in the earth (verse 7).

How do we go about making sure we give God no rest? We do it by putting prayer first. Preaching is altogether hopeless unless it is supported by prayer. Ask yourself this telling question: apart perhaps from the usual weekly prayer meeting, have you spent some time last night or this very morning in prayer? We have to come to a place of practical immediacy, but it takes a long time to get there. We try this; we try that; we get excited about one scheme and another, but still the people perish. We should be yearning for that time when the people of God shall arise to do no other than declare the unsearchable riches of Christ. The result of that would be that heaven would come down, multitudes would believe, and holiness and God's glory would fill the length and breadth of the land. We must break our guilty silence and we must prevail in prayer!

A very famous hymn by Charles Wesley will illustrate further my meaning. The hymn is based on the story of Jacob at Peniel. Beautifully written and very searching, it begins:

> Come, O Thou Traveller unknown,
> Whom still I hold, but cannot see!
> My company before is gone,
> And I am left alone with Thee;
> With Thee all night I mean to stay,
> And wrestle till the break of day.

Do you remember what Jacob had done? He was a very crafty man, very much like you and me in his cunning. At this particular time in his life, he was, in fact, to all intents and purposes, facing extinction. So what he decided—very wisely—to do, in order to better the chances of survival, was to divide his family into two separate units. Having done this, what he did next was to venture himself into the presence of his God. He was alone with God. And so it is with us: we must learn not only to support the prayer meeting, but also to know what it is to be alone with God. This is, for example, something which tells immediately in our preaching or in our disposition to witness. Eloquence has nothing to do with it. It is so obvious when a man has been alone with God and has come to that all important understanding and familiarity with spiritual things. Wesley's hymn goes on:

> I need not tell Thee who I am,
>   My misery and sin declare;
>   Thyself hast called me by my name;
>   Look on Thy hands, and read it there:
>   But who, I ask Thee, who art Thou?
>   Tell me Thy Name, and tell me now.

In a way, spiritually, we also can be in that position in which we do not yet fully know His name, in that place where we have not yet come to experience and fathom all that God is willing to reveal to us of Himself at that particular time. The seeking must go on:

> In vain Thou strugglest to get free;
>   I never will unloose my hold!
>   Art thou the Man that died for me?
>   The secret of Thy love unfold:
>   Wrestling, I will not let Thee go,
>   Till I Thy Name, Thy nature know.

Can you feel and appreciate something of what it means to wrestle like this with God? There is an old fashioned phrase which we would do well to reintroduce in this present day. To spend time *agonizing in prayer* would, in the minds of our forefathers, most certainly have been considered worthwhile, if not an absolutely necessary requirement, in order to achieve the blessing—a prayer that hurts and in a sense, becomes almost unbearable until finally there is a breakthrough, and all is turned to joy!

What though my shrinking flesh complain,
And murmur to contend so long?
I rise superior to my pain,
When I am weak, then I am strong;
And when my all of strength shall fail,
I shall with the God-Man prevail.

Yield to me now; for I am weak,
But confident in self-despair;
Speak to my heart, in blessings speak,
Be conquered by my instant prayer;
Speak, or Thou never hence shalt move,
And tell me if Thy Name is Love.

Then, of course, if you remember the story, Jacob is dealt with: he is made lame. In the actual account, the breaking was physical, but there is also a spiritual breaking, a lameness in the soul, which is of God. Have we experienced this? Do we know what it is to be broken?

Contented now upon my thigh
I halt, till life's short journey end;
All helplessness, all weakness, I
On Thee alone for strength depend;
Nor have I power from Thee to move:
Thy nature and Thy Name is Love.

Do we know anything about the kind of prayer and preaching that produces this? Can we not come to the Lord and ask Him what we should do? Can we not ask Him to enable us to lift the cross of Jesus Christ and glorify His Name? Can we not ask Him for power to preach the blood of our Lord and Saviour Jesus Christ while, at the same time, still be unashamed and unembarrassed by its simplicity?

What else is there for us to consider? We are, of course, not to forget that we are also called upon always to pray through the service on a normal Sabbath's day. We are to pray that the preacher's arms may be upheld and Israel prevail. Then, also, when we go to the normal weekly prayer meeting, our aim there again will be to meet with God. Evan Roberts, one of God's instruments in the 1904 Welsh Revival, when inquiring about a prayer meeting, did not ask, as we so often do, how many people were present or was it good or how many prayed. His question was never about those things at all, but rather his desire was to know to what degree the actual presence of God was granted in that meeting. Praying is meeting with God's own Person. We pray, we seek, we plead, we wrestle, and we argue until we are actually given audience with the most High. Having been granted such a privilege, what we do then is not so much to persist any longer with our own wishes but rather to listen to and subject ourselves to His.

Marcus Rainsford has a lovely way of describing this particular aspect of prayer. In his book, *Our Lord Prays for His Own*, he bids us consider this most important truth: prayer is not changing the heart of God, for His heart is already inclined; prayer is presenting to God His own promises and claiming these promises that they may be fulfilled by faith. Prayer, then, is essentially the laying before God of His own promises.

In Oswald Sanders' booklet *Effective Prayer*, published by the old China Inland Mission, now the Overseas Missionary Fellowship, it is put like this: "A promise by God is a pledge by God. It provides the warrant and forms the basis of the prayer of faith. The stability of a promise rests upon the character and resources of the One who makes it, even as the value of a check depends upon the honesty and resources of the one who signs it. The character and fidelity of God vouch for the credibility of the promises He makes. . . . With God, promise and performance are inseparable. But promises must be distinguished from facts. We accept a stated fact of God's

Word, but we plead a promise. When God proclaims a fact, faith accepts and acts upon it. When God makes a promise, we comply with its conditions, claim its fulfillment, and receive the promised favor. The function of the prayer of faith is to turn God's promises into facts of experience. The patriarchs through faith obtained the fulfillment of God's promises (Hebrews 11:33) and turned them into personal experience. The prayer of faith has its basis in neither outward circumstances nor inward feelings. It is when sight brings no helpful vision and comfortable emotions are largely absent that the prayer of faith finds its greatest opportunity. It springs from the naked promise or affirmation of the Word of God, for faith proceeds only from a divine warrant. The prayer of faith is the power which converts promise into performance."

Such potential as this is too valuable to be passed by, neglected, or forgotten. We must seek its fulfillment. Admittedly, to try to comprehend and, still further, apply these principles is difficult for the very reason that they represent some of the most profound aspects of the spiritual life. They are the hardest things of all for flesh and self to have to grapple with, yet grapple we must. Perhaps we think that we have been very good in these things already, good merely because we go dutifully, regularly every week to the prayer meeting. We can almost hear ourselves talking—"Oh yes, I've been to the prayer meeting. It was very good, but I didn't pray—I was too shy." Really, what kind of talk is that? It is not the voice of someone who has seen the need for revival. If we cannot pray in public yet, all well and good, but if we will not pray, we should be ashamed of ourselves. Oh, my soul, that thou wouldst discover anew the promises of God and, like the patriarchs of old, take hold of them and lay them before God! Promise yourself that you will not let Him go until He blesses you. Seek this tremendous, heroic, effective dimension of prayer. Settle for no less.

As a source of encouragement for us, God's answer and decision with respect to Isaiah's prayer is outlined in verses eight and nine:

> The Lord hath sworn by His right hand, and by the arm of His strength, Surely I will no more give thy corn to be meat for thine enemies; and the sons of the stranger shall not drink thy wine, for the which thou hast laboured: But they that have gathered it shall eat it, and praise the Lord; and they that have brought it together shall drink it in the courts of My holiness.

The main thought of these two verses is this: God shall give His presence to His people, and the good things and privileges which rightly belong to them shall no longer be given to others as punishment to them. Notice also another interesting element: His desire, is in fact, to always give us more than our sensed present need and to grant us the blessing by degrees. He will, if you like, grant us as much as we can bear of the presence of God at any one time. What comfort there is in His measured dealings with us! What perfect condescension He shows to suit our frailties and meet our needs!

> Without Thy presence, King of Saints,
> Our purpose fails, our spirit faints.
> Joseph Tritton

How true and how very real always is our present need of Him to sustain our very hearts and souls. Isn't it wonderful, therefore, that we can indeed turn to Him for these things? Do it now if you have such a desire. Ask Him to grant such a sense of His presence that we might know that we are sheep of His pasture and know Him as our God. He will then encourage us to go on. He has told us that He will give us preachers, stir us up to pray, and teach us something about this prevailing prayer.

While these are His promises, in all of this we must give Him
our generous co-operation. Lead us on, Lord, because the need
is great!

> Go through, go through the gates; prepare ye the way of
> the people; cast up, cast up the highway; gather out the
> stones; lift up a standard for the people (verse 10).

Here, it is as if He has got a picture of Zion in all her desolation, but suddenly things begin to change, and as the change is
taking place, He wants us now to undertake to clear a great
highway. In order to do it, we must gather up the stones. It was
once a clear highway, but today there are rocks of resistance in
our hearts, stones of prejudice. We want to sin a little, then
pray a little. We want to enjoy a little, then seek a little. When
will we ever learn? Our uncertain lives are even now rapidly
fading away like a vapor; before we know it, we will be no
more. Why can't we call upon Him now while He is near?
Why can't we seek with all our hearts while He can yet be
found?

I can remember reading at the age of fourteen the account
of the 1859 revival in the old Cymru Coch Welsh magazines
belonging to my grandparents. Although an unconverted boy at
the time, I still recall being completely taken up by the thrilling
thought of God intervening in the affairs of His Church at a
particular time and in a particular place—God, as it were,
invading His own people and, at the same time, a whole area
being overwhelmed and drawn to these great things; God,
having become weary of the chaos, deciding upon a radical,
supernatural divine solution; God Himself coming into the
midst of the preaching to make it a living thing, into the midst
of prayer so that supplication would prevail and intercession
succeed, into the midst of Zion so that men even outside Zion
might know Him and come in. How I used to long for it then!
How I still long for it even to this day! I have known men who

all their lives have prayed earnestly that they might see this before they died, but were not given that privilege. It may be that to them was granted another, different privilege, that privilege of being with those of God's people who were allowed to go to Mount Nebo and look upon the land beyond—a privilege indeed in its own right, and yet it is still not all that we would seek for from our God.

Once more, let us seriously address ourselves in this matter. Do we really want this desolation and dearth to continue, just meeting occasionally here and there, desperately trying to encourage one another? How much better it would be if our village, town, or city had new gatherings of people such as we previously would never have dreamed possible: three or four meetings perhaps on the Sundays and still the congregations not satisfied even with that! Such a situation would prove beyond doubt that there had indeed been a move from God. Alternatively it might be described as something which had happened also in the hearts and souls of ministers, elders, and even ordinary Christians, many of them never having spoken like this before. See, therefore, what the Lord can do!

Dear reader, stir up your faith and believe in this great God. Begin with your own self! Have you a stony heart? Are you perhaps really tense even as you read these things? Deep down do you know that without Him you cannot really change anything, whereas with Him you know that all things are possible? Search your own heart!

> Search me, O God, and know my heart: try me, and know my thoughts: And see if there be any wicked way in me, and lead me in the way everlasting (Psalm 139:23-24).

Do this, Lord, so that I might enter into this teaching and into this prayer and into this consecration. When the Church does finally agree to venture along this path its reward is very great indeed. As Isaiah 62:11 indicates:

> Behold, the Lord hath proclaimed unto the end of the world, Say ye to the daughter of Zion, Behold, thy salvation cometh; behold, His reward is with Him, and His work before Him.

The revived Church is so enlarged that we can hardly imagine it.

Have you ever heard or read about the work that God has done in reviving His Church in Korea? That Church, because of revival, is today immensely large; the size of one congregation alone is measured in tens of thousands. If we are a hundred or so, we are inclined to think that we are too many! We are very small-minded. How can we allow ourselves to think in that way? Does it not grieve us to think of the multitudes hurtling hellward? Does not this instill agony in your heart? With a view to the destiny of souls, we have no right to neglect our responsibility. As far as we are concerned, we must preach the Gospel to every creature; this is our mandate and ought also to be the very burden of our hearts.

When revival comes, we change. We may not like the change. We shall become a holy people. Nowadays, we would rather be called a happy people, but in that day—in the day of revival—if asked how did the service go, the people will not answer, "I was made happy" or "I was entertained" or "I participated," but they will tell rather of how they have been moved of God.

> And they shall call them, The holy people, The redeemed of the Lord: and thou shalt be called, Sought out, A city not forsaken (verse 12).

May God grant this prophecy fulfillment again in our own day and age. We see a Church which is today in need, forsaken, and desolate but some day soon, hopefully, to be revived to its full and former glory—a Church restored in the true and real meaning of the word. What then is our responsibility meanwhile? God is telling us to make clear the highway of our hearts, to enter with thanksgiving into Zion, with no prejudices that are a hindrance to the work of the Spirit within us. And then what will it be like when revival does come at last?

A missionary, writing about the Korean revival of 1907, vividly describes one incident as follows: "At Monday noon, we missionaries met and cried out to God in earnest. We were bound in spirit and refused to let God go till He blessed us. That night it was very different. Each felt as he entered the church that the room was full of God's Presence. Not only missionaries but Koreans testified to the same thing . . . After a short sermon, Mr. Lee took charge of the meeting and called for prayers. So many began praying that Mr. Lee said, 'If you want to pray like that, all pray,' and the whole congregation began to pray out loud, all together. The effect was indescribable—not confusion, but a vast harmony of sound and spirit, a mingling together of souls moved by an irresistible impulse of prayer. The prayer sounded to me like the falling of many waters, an ocean of prayer beating against God's throne. . . . He came to us in Pyengyang that night with the sound of weeping. As the prayer continued, a spirit of heaviness and sorrow for sin came down upon the congregation. . . . Man after man would rise, confess his sins, break down and weep, and then throw himself to the floor and beat the floor with his fists in perfect agony of conviction. . . . Sometimes after a confession the whole congregation would break out in audible prayer. . . . Again, after another confession, they would break out in uncontrollable weeping, and we would all weep; we could not help it. And so the meeting went on until two o'clock in the morning, with confession and weeping and praying."

"Ah well," you might say, "that's Korea." Consider then another account, in another place, in another time, yet still well within living memory. Duncan Campbell's biographer writes about the year 1949, describing the Isle of Lewis: "A solemn hush came over the church the following night when Duncan Campbell turned this time to *the foolish virgins*. The service closed in a tense silence and the building emptied. As he came down from the pulpit a young deacon raised his hand and moving it in a circle above his head whispered: 'Mr. Campbell, God is hovering over, He is going to break through. I can hear already the rumbling of heaven's chariot-wheels. . . .' The entire congregation was lingering outside, reluctant to disperse; others had joined them, drawn from their homes by an irresistible power they had not experienced before. There were looks of deep distress on many faces. Suddenly a cry pierced the silence; a young man who had remained in the church, burdened to the point of agony for his fellow-men, was pouring out his desire in prayer. He was so overcome that he fell into a trance and, as he lay prostrate on the floor, the congregation swept back into the church. The awful presence of God brought a wave of conviction of sin that caused even mature Christians to feel their sinfulness, bringing groans of distress and prayers of repentance from the unconverted. Strong men were bowed under the weight of sin and cries for mercy were mingled with shouts of joy from others who passed into life."

Do we believe such a thing as this can really happen? Is there the slightest possibility that we can now, today, grasp this precious promise by faith? When we look at the desolation and irreligion, our hearts almost faint within us thinking we could never change anything even if we knew where to start, what to say, or what to do. We know at this present time, in this spiritual environment, if we were to stand on a street corner and plead with the people, they would mostly pass us by. Yet, we still hold to this conviction with our very lives—change can again happen, wrought in that time when we enter into that arena of God's blessing, when God again gives Himself afresh to be with His people. Philip Doddridge was privileged to witness the beginnings of the eighteenth century revival in England. Contemplating the possibilities for change then unfolding, he wrote with hope and confidence, expecting great things from God and for His Church:

> Triumphant Zion, lift thy head
> From dust and ashes and the dead;
> Thou, humbled long, awake at length,
> And gird thee with thy Saviour's strength.
>
> Put all thy beauteous garments on,
> And let thine excellence be known;
> Decked in the robes of righteousness,
> The world thy glories shall confess.
>
> No more shall foes unclean invade,
> And fill thy hallowed walls with dread;
> No more shall hell's insulting host
> Their victory and thy sorrows boast.
>
> God from on high has heard thy prayer;
> His hand thy ruins shall repair;
> Reared and adorned by love divine
> Thy towers and battlements shall shine.
>
> Grace shall dispose my heart and voice
> To share and echo back her joys;
> Nor will thy watchful Monarch cease
> To guard thee in eternal peace.

Another hymn, another witness, another expectant note:

The day of Thy grace is at hand
To tell and to trust in Thy Name,
Thy righteousness stands to command
Thine honour and glory and fame.

No more shall Jerusalem mourn,
Nor heaviness wear them that weep,
His beauty for ashes will turn
The contrite, their Saviour to greet.

The spirit of praise shall be heard
In Zion, the city of God,
Proclaiming the truth of His Word,
Good tidings their tongues sound abroad.

Forsaken, forgotten no more
And stark desolation they spurn,
Delight of the Lord, oh restore
Her lamp of salvation to burn.

Prepare, Oh prepare for the day
The glory of God will appear,
Prepare, Oh prepare now the way;
Dispel from your hearts every fear.

Oh Sought Out, and cherished by grace,
Go through, Oh go through His great gates,
And enter with worship, and raise
His standard, and hold His dictates.

The need is great, admittedly so, but do we not see also how this need is surrounded by the promises of God? Forsaken we are! But can this be His lasting desire for us? Surely not! Do not His own person and character suggest otherwise? Of course they do! Let us then lay hold on the promises and seek Him!

Chapter 2

THE CRY FOR REVIVAL
(Isaiah 63)

In Isaiah sixty-two we became aware both of Jerusalem's need and also that of the Church of Jesus Christ. We discovered something of the immense love and great plan that God has for His Church—that He does not desire Jerusalem, as representing the Church of God, to be forsaken but rather that she should be the very delight of the Lord. There is much with which we can identify in this chapter. There is a need which cannot but be there when we consider our own land and the desolation that surrounds us. If we care at all about the Church of Jesus Christ and the continuance of the work of the Gospel, we cannot but be sorely concerned. Although we have a joy in the Lord, we feel a great sorrow when we see things as they are today. Sadness fills our hearts when we see peoples and nations ruling their affairs as if there were no God. Indeed, even we ourselves often live so close to the way of the world that it seems sometimes as if we, too, have forgotten our God in the midst of the great decline that has taken place.

Also in Isaiah sixty-two, we noticed that the prophet was a man completely taken up, consumed, with a concern for the honor of God. While there is obviously concern for the Church, for Jerusalem, and for the people, there is also apparent an overriding and divine jealousy, desiring above all else that the name of God should be honored. Revivals are times when God honors His own name in just such a way; a time in which the name of Jesus Christ is glorified and exalted; a time during which He becomes revered among men; a time when something of the loveliness of God is made known. It is such a view of Christ, for example, as that described in Toplady's hymn, which did indeed at one time, in the singing of it, convey this very blessing by the Spirit's hand to my own soul. I well remember the experience of being caught up with the wonder of it all, the desires of my heart centering upon the:

> Object of my first desire,
> Jesus crucified for me;
> All to happiness aspire,
> Only to be found in Thee:
> Thee to praise, and Thee to know,
> Constitute my bliss below;
> Thee to see, and Thee to love,
> Constitute my bliss above.

He goes on:

> Lord, it is not life to live
> If Thy presence Thou deny;

What a statement! I wonder how many of us can venture to declare that we have come to a similar position in our own experience? Being completely satisfied with Him alone, so that we are able to say:

> Lord, if Thou Thy presence give,
> 'Tis no longer death to die:
> Source and giver of repose,
> Singly from Thy smile it flows;
> Peace and happiness are Thine;
> Mine they are, if Thou art mine.

We come now to Isaiah sixty-three, in the course of which we move on from the description of the need expressed by the prophet to that which might be termed the cry of the prophet. It is unfortunate but true that a person can be aware of the spiritual need in a particular land and yet fall short of responding correctly to that need. A person might just say, "Well, that's all very interesting and what a pity," and then think nothing more of it. Similarly, someone reading a book containing church statistics might well say, "Dear me, I had not imagined that things had declined that far," and then resign himself to a position of apathy. Yet, on the other hand, I believe that if we had a real conception of the devastation that has been wrought in our one-time Christian country, this fair land of Wales, once known as the *Land of Revival*, we would not dismiss so easily what the enemy has done. Sometimes I think that we in Wales still aspire and still attempt to draw consolations today from blessings long gone past. Let us get this one point clear once and for all: Wales has no monopoly on revival. It is not exclusively our prerogative; far from it! As most of my quotations deliberately show, other lands have had and some are even now enjoying revival, while we are not.

What does the word *revival* mean to you? Does it mean excitement? Does it mean everybody jumping about and making a fuss? You may have an impression of revival which is not revival at all. Or perhaps you have heard about the confessions of sin made under the power of God, and that has terrified you. You may be saying, "I don't want that at all! I don't want to be a public spectacle." What you have heard maybe are snippets here and there, enough to frighten you away and make you think that revival must be some kind of strange, freakish phenomenon.

True revival is not like that at all. Anything and everything that God does is good, and revival is most definitely something that God does. It comes from Him. It is God's very best given to His people. Sometimes, because revival may be such a long time coming, we can be tempted to despair and say, "Ah! It will not come in my time, so I will go for God's second best and choose meanwhile to busy myself with all kinds of activities." These self efforts are sometimes good, often tiring, and usually need a great deal of energy and organization. Revival is different. It is <u>God's</u> intervention, very often following on and taking over after man's exasperation. Sometimes revival comes when there has been a great dearth, when it seems as if the embers, the very last sparks of religion, are dying on the hearth; it is then that He comes, breaking in from above, unsought. There are other times when men have been seeking it with all their hearts, when they have been inspired to do so by God, and yet still when He comes, it will be by His sovereign will. There are yet other times, times perhaps when persecution is on the way; in such times, God can again come and prepare His Church to meet the trial by granting her a great and powerful revival. In any of these instances, revival may come to a single church or to a particular area or to a whole nation or nations, and it lasts for as long as our sovereign God decrees.

Revival is something above and beyond that spiritual environment and climate which we, for want of a better word, would deem normal. In aspiring to greater things, we are in no way belittling that which we already enjoy. In non-revival times we give ourselves to hear the exposition of His Word and apply it to our souls. We also desire that, by His Spirit, we can apply it to our lives. When we sing a hymn of praise and worship to God, it rises as a sweet incense if we do so in spirit and in truth. We live day to day in the power of His Spirit. These are great and wonderful things, in no way to be decried. We are able to say now that we are deeply satisfied with these gifts from God. Yet in revival there is something more; there is that great plus which in no way dishonors God's present dealings with us when we seek it, which can neither be faked nor substituted nor bypassed once we have set our hearts upon it. Once we have appreciated and tasted its potential, nothing else will do. That is the highest plane of spiritual experience, the ultimate that God can do for His people in this world. You may have become slowly aware of its reality in your reading of church history or, more blessed still, by being present in an actual revival or perhaps by visiting a place where you can catch the aftermath of one. Many have testified that breathing the air of revival in this manner is enough to create a yearning for it which is never stilled until satisfied by the granting of it again.

What is revival? It is another dimension, in which tremendous things happen and God's people are at last moved. William B. Sprague summarized some of its major aspects and manifestations as follows:

1. There Is a Revival of Scriptural Knowledge — People really come to know their Bibles and, when they pray, a wealth of scriptural passages and verses weave through their prayers. Compare this to the poverty that there is in our prayer life today. During times of revival almost every other sentence would probably contain some Scripture. The revival of scriptural knowledge would also mean its application in people's lives. A knowledge of the promises of God would be used in order that those promises be claimed.

2. There Is a Revival of Vital Piety — By this is meant not just pietism—in a sense that would be obnoxious—but rather true godliness: godly men and women clearly identifiable, found throughout all congregations in the various towns and regions in which we live.

3. There Is a Revival of Practical Obedience — People say that revival is impractical and other-worldly, but of course, it is not. Revival brings an abundance of change to every avenue of society: improvements, blessings, side-effects, which are by-products of the one central movement. You cannot begin by improving the periphery, you must begin with God. You start at the center in order to see the results spread eventually to the corners. It is then that people's lives are healed. It is then that those people who had never previously considered God find themselves seeking a place of worship. This is revival.

How is it all brought about? It is here that we have to begin to say something about the preaching during times of revival. There is such a thing as preaching in the power of the Spirit. John Elias of Anglesey, during one of the Welsh awakenings, is recorded to have preached in Rhuddlan on the steps of the New Inn at the time of the winter fair. What followed gives us some idea of the impact of revival preaching. By all accounts, it was a rough and dangerous fair to frequent—even murder was but a small thing in the eyes of the thronging, greedy money-makers. A small group of anxious Christians had gathered themselves around John Elias as he preached on the keeping of the Sabbath day. He applied his message by shouting out, "Thieves!" He shouted it seven times, his voice rising as he did so, with the startling result that some of the people literally began to faint under the conviction of sin. It is said that following this incident the fair did not restart for decades. The impact of the event was so considerable that a commemorative mug was struck in a place so far afield as the potteries district of England. On one side of that particular mug the view was that of riotous living, while on the other, by contrast, was a portrayal of the penitents, coupled with an explanatory reference to the preaching of John Elias at Rhuddlan. Such obvious and lasting influence as this cannot be attained other than by God's own presence. You or I could presumably decide to be brave and stand before a public house and begin to preach, but we would be fools to do it unless we had a real assurance that it was God who had sent us. That alone would result in revival.

When God is with us in this way, our preaching, behavior, prayer, and worship all take on a completely new dimension. Chapels would begin to fill, people would increasingly find themselves sitting or standing in the aisles and on the pulpit steps, and very soon even the preacher would have to struggle to find a place to put his feet! There would perhaps be crowds gathering outside the building, and once again the old provision of carving out doors behind the pulpit in order to enable the minister to get in would have to be repeated! Men and women who previously had never given religion a second thought would be struck down in the midst of their folly, first seeking and then finding God. They would at last begin to take God seriously, filling prayer meetings and Bible classes, and thereby ensuring that the Lord Jesus Christ is glorified.

There is an incident recorded in Tregaron when M.P. Morgan, a much respected saint of God who was many times used in revival, gave his text from the Song of Solomon. As soon as he had done so, suddenly and without warning, a lady stood up and broke out with these words, *O Rosyn, Rhosyn Saron!* (*Oh Rose, Rose of Sharon!*) and as she said it again spontaneously, the whole congregation found itself weeping. Intermingled with the weeping could be heard the ejaculation of praise being repeated many times over, *Rhosyn Saron! Ti yw tegwch nef y nef, ar ddeng mil y mae'n rhagori!* (*Rose of Sharon! You are foremost in all the heavens, chief among ten thousand!*) These words became text and sermon for the day. It went on for hours: glimpses of the Saviour granted, as we have touched upon already, in the aftermath of revival; beautiful things, worth seeking and cherishing if ever you have the opportunity to experience them.

The incidents recorded are very, very many. I will give you yet another, this time from my own family history. In 1904, when my mother was a child, my grandfather was a quarry worker in Llanberis, at which work place he, like many others, was forced to lodge during the weekdays and then walk eight or nine miles home to Caernarfon every weekend. On arriving home after a meal, he would go immediately to the Saturday night fellowship meeting and then the following day to the Sunday services. This he would do regularly, always in this committed fashion. Then one Saturday night there appeared more commitment even than that which was usual. At eleven p.m., my grandfather came running home from chapel, and immediately my grandmother commented on his lateness. "No," he said, "I am not late, we are only just getting started. Hurry up, girl!" "Hold on, I have a child in my arms!" she said. "Bring the child along," he answered. And so they both went at eleven o'clock with the child to attend the praising and worshipping of God. Doing this, they never seemed to get tired, and all the while they continued to do their daily work without detriment. They were carried on the crest of this great wave of the presence of God, all the while glorifying Christ. This glorifying of Christ is in fact one of the most marvelous aspects of revival. Revival is a work of the Holy Spirit, the work of the Spirit being that of glorifying the Son of God with the result that His Name once again becomes revered upon the lips of men and women.

Let us take another example, this time from the 1859 Revival in Northern Ireland. One particularly memorable experience is described as follows: "We had been praying for and expecting some such precious blessing, but were, notwithstanding, taken by surprise, so sudden, powerful, and extraordinary were the manifestations of the Spirit's presence. Persons of every shade of temperament and character were mysteriously affected, overpowered, prostrated, and made to pour out the most thrilling, agonizing cries for mercy. Most of those thus impressed and awakened found peace and comfort in a very short space of time, and then their countenances shone with sweetness and glory beyond description. Very many of them received a marvelous fluency and power of prayer. A hatred of sin, a love for the Saviour, a zeal for His cause, an affection for one another, and an anxiety about perishing sinners took absolute possession of their hearts and literally ruled and governed their actions. For about six weeks, almost all agricultural operations and, indeed, every kind of secular employment was suspended, no man being able to think of or attend to anything but the interests of his soul. Night and day the sound of praise and prayer never ceased to float upon the air. An overwhelming sense of awe and terror held in check the boldest sinners, while thousands who till now had lived as if eternity was a fiction seemed now for the first time to realize its truth and presence, and to feel as if the end of all things was at hand. I should say about one thousand people were suddenly, sensibly and powerfully impressed and awakened."

These descriptions speak for themselves. I recall reading about the same 1859 revival in Wales when I was a boy of about fourteen. I can well remember being totally captivated in my own imagination at that time. Although unconverted, I was later to venture into the ministry still thinking only of revival, greatly concerned that revival might not break out before my college course had ended! Yet since that time, the years have gone by and still no revival. Yes, there is rejoicing for what God has given to our various little congregations, and for the converts, but O Lord, we really had expected more than this! In the same way as the prospect gripped my soul as a young boy, oh! that the prospect would grip us again!

Let me take a further incident from the 1859 revival in Wales. At one particular time during that revival, everywhere in the immediate district surrounding the town of Dolgellau, there were people rejoicing and praising, singing and, during the meetings, filling all the chapels. Dolgellau town itself, however, still remained as dead as could be, even though its chapels also were full of people pleading, praying, and agonizing. What eventually happened? The deadlock in the end was broken by children! The account given was that one night they decided to sneak out of bed, somehow managing to get the key to the minister's vestry, the *inner sanctum*, a place forbidden to children in a time when elders were elders! They proceeded to put papers over the windows and in the keyholes so that no one would catch them. They then lit a candle and began to pray. What should they do? They felt terrible that revival had not come to their town and began to plead with God. The eldest, who was only twelve, led with the words, *Ein Tad yr Hwn wyt yn y nefoedd, sancteiddien Dy Enw, delen dy deyrnas. (Our Father which art in heaven, hallowed be Thy name, Thy kingdom come.)* It was the only prayer he knew, in response to which, nevertheless, God did indeed come! The children had crept gingerly through the cemetery, terrified of every grave, but now they flung open the doors and windows, jumping and leaping over the gravestones as they went out. As they did so, the people of Dolgellau came to meet them, proclaiming, "He has come!" Such is what happens in revival! Can you try a little to comprehend the totally different dimension that is thereby involved? Such a thing as this cannot be organized in any way whatsoever. You cannot suddenly decide to rush out of the house at twelve-thirty a.m. and say, "He has come!" It just does not happen like that. It is rather, indeed, it has to be, therefore, a spontaneous, glorious, supernatural event, being no less than an actual visitation from God Himself.

Oh, that we in this present generation might be caught up in such a visitation at least once before our era draws to a close! Meanwhile, our solemn duty is to preach the Gospel. Preacher of God, preacher of the Word, you must preach the blood, the forgiveness of sins, repentance and faith. But above all else, God wants watchmen who will prevail in prayer, congregations, also, that know how to pray, how to pray through vital issues concerning life and death and the salvation of souls. What God wants are congregations that know how to pray for their pastors that they be given enabling power to succeed in the work that God has given them.

How do we begin to pray along such lines? Most importantly, pray first of all that there might be not only a sense of the presence of God but also that the minister might be able to bear it. Tackle these things on a spiritual level. Begin to pray on a higher dimension. It is so easy to look at the present need and say, "Revival? It has been such a long time, and the tide has gone out so far. Surely it will never come back in again. This is an advanced century: the age of the video, television, and computers. The tide has gone out too far, and it will go out still further; sin will become bolder; heresy and confusion will reign supreme. The world already behaves as if God were dead and His children forsaken. Can we still believe that it is God's intention not to leave us desolate, that we are indeed the delight of His soul, and that He desires for us to be revived from the very depth of His innermost being, far more so than that degree which we desire for ourselves?" What is our verdict in these things?

It is so easy to relax and rock away in our evangelical rocking chairs. Do you have an evangelical rocking chair? Do you know all your doctrines, and are you content that you are sound, perfectly and wonderfully sound? The chair is sound, and you are rocking beautifully. You have read, chewed, and swallowed Berkhof's *Systematic Theology*, digested perhaps twenty-two volumes of Calvin, along with a host of others! Very good, you should not be ignorant, but how can we rock so comfortably amidst all our knowledge and still not apply it? In contrast, there is also the experimental rocking chair. "I was in such a place, and I experienced this, that, and the other, and now I am so contented, satisfied, and comfortable that I can hardly make a move at all." Present-day Christian believer, we must cease to rock, We must get out of our chairs and get on our knees before God. Of course we must honor the doctrines, and there are also many experiences which will remain to us always precious. But beware! Beware of presumption and sloth! Beware also of that which awaits you if you do begin to awake from your slumbers!

Once you come to that place where you know God can intervene and you are determined to be both evangelical and spiritual, it is then that your adversary the devil will begin to take notice. Be prepared for this. He may well whisper in your ear, "All this is just Welsh sentiment—1904 and all that." Take heed, for the devil, as always, is a liar. In this he lies: he lies for the simple reason that revivals are not exclusively *Welsh* preserves; still less are they "past it" in terms of the wider world historical perspective. On the contrary, revivals are still going on today in many different locations across the globe, and if the Lord tarries, there will surely be more. Yet we must recognize that there is an adversary, Satan, who does not want the people of these islands to begin again to worship God. Satan does not want people to honor God in their everyday pursuits, so as to begin to affect and permeate society. He will do everything he can to persuade us that these things are impractical in our century, saying that God will have a more intellectual or mechanical way of working, using the talents, gifts, and machinery that men have today. We must not listen to him. Revival has always been, and still remains, God's essential tool for moving the hearts of men. Revival changes lives; it changes history. It is the *vision* without which *the people perish* (Proverbs 29:18).

At the beginning of Isaiah sixty-three, there is both a picture and a question: "Who is this that cometh from Edom, with dyed garments from Bozrah?" Liberal commentators would say that this is probably an interpolation, which means it should not be there. Yet in my Bible, it is there, and I am glad it is because God here is holding something very wonderful before our eyes. He is turning our attention towards the Saviour. This Saviour has been on a campaign to Bozrah which was the capital of Edom. Edom here represents all that which is opposed to the work of God. Let us consider the paragraph in full:

> Who is this that cometh from Edom, with dyed garments from Bozrah? this that is glorious in His apparel, travelling in the greatness of His strength? I that speak in righteousness, mighty to save. Wherefore art Thou red in Thine apparel, and Thy garments like him that treadeth in the winefat? I have trodden the winepress alone; and of the people there was none with Me: for I will tread them in Mine anger, and trample them in My

fury; and their blood shall be sprinkled upon My garments, and I will stain all My raiment. For the day of vengeance is in Mine heart, and the year of My redeemed is come. And I looked, and there was none to help; and I wondered that there was none to uphold: therefore Mine own arm brought salvation unto Me; and My fury, it upheld Me. And I will tread down the people in Mine anger, and make them drunk in My fury, and I will bring down their strength to the earth (verses 1-6).

What is it exactly that we have represented here? Let us take another related verse from the Book of Revelation using the same imagery, Revelation 19:13: "And He was clothed with a vesture dipped in blood: and His name is called The Word of God." Who is He? He is both the *mighty warrior* and the one who is *altogether lovely*, returning victoriously from having struck at the heart of the enemy's stronghold—that place which represents Satan with all his powers and principalities. He is none other than my Lord and Saviour Jesus Christ. What has He done? His garments are dipped in blood; He has paid the penalty for my sin; He has purchased for me repentance and faith, by means of which I now belong to Him. He has triumphed over Satan and is victor over the grave! He also will be judge over all! Yes, that aspect is yet to come. God reminds us here that He will certainly judge, indeed, that Christ will judge in righteousness so that we His saints might fear Him. Do we then, therefore, take heed of Isaiah's exhortations? If there are any of us who have not, should we not do it now?

> Turn your eyes upon Jesus,
> Look full in His wonderful face;
> And the things of earth will grow strangely dim
> In the light of His glory and grace.
>   H. H. Lemmel

See Him there then, our Lord and Saviour Jesus Christ. Why is it that we always address Him with His titles in that order? It is for the reason that He was Lord before He became our Saviour. He always has been Lord; now He has become the Saviour; and as we turn our gaze upon Him, it is to be ransomed, healed, restored and forgiven.

Let us return to the text and see how it is that God's people are dealt with in this manner:

> I will mention the lovingkindnesses of the Lord, and the praises of the Lord, according to all that the Lord hath bestowed on us, and the great goodness toward the house of Israel, which He hath bestowed on them according to His mercies, and according to the multitude of His loving-kindnesses (verse 7).

We begin with this great vision of God bringing home to His people an abundance of tender mercies and loving-kindnesses. Here is manifestation and proof of God's mercy, resting on His redemptive love.

Assurance follows:

> For he said, Surely they are My people, children that will not lie: so He was their Saviour (verse 8).

I wonder if the wonderful blessings here described are true of you? You say, "Yes, they are!" So then He is your Saviour also? He is, indeed, if you have come to an experience of the grace of God where God has granted you faith to believe and holy sorrow not to be repented of. He is your Saviour if you have been quickened by the Holy Spirit, have thrown yourself upon the mercy of Christ, and have known the experience of sins forgiven. It is then, and only then, that you are able to say, "Yes indeed, I surely am one of His people."

In John seventeen we are given a particularly lovely description of what has befallen us if we have become Christians: we have, as it were, become no less than the Father's own gifts to His Son. What *presents* are these? Gifts of the Father, washed, cleansed, given to Jesus, and now exalted in the sight of God. How He must love us! Listen to how this love is described:

> In all their affliction He was afflicted, and the angel of His presence saved them: in His love and in His pity He redeemed them; and He bare them, and carried them all the days of old (verse 9).

Incomparable love, as always, is this love which is in the bosom of God. Meditating again on John seventeen, we see, in His prayer for us, our blessed Saviour asking that the same measure of love which the Father has towards the Son might also be reflected in the love that God has towards us. Behold what manner, what degree and depth and quality of love the Father hath bestowed upon us! We are now the sons of God. We are His people and the sheep of His pasture, and He that comes from Edom is our Saviour. Oh that we might be given more grace to appreciate Him!

So we continue in this majestic sixty-third chapter by maintaining that what we have in it is God giving to us the "angel of his presence" (verse 9). Oh, that He might do that in the same special way in our generation! Oh, that we might be able to say, "Christ Himself has come, in the very angel of His presence," in that dimension whereby He grants us such a vision of Himself that we cannot and will not be satisfied with anything less! I myself have never experienced a revival first hand, but I have had the privilege of visiting a place still glowing and bathed in the aftermath of one, and that experience in and of itself has totally convinced me that we should never be satisfied with anything other than God's best.

May I illustrate further? Despite the limitations of my physical constitution, I was once a coal miner! One experience which I had working below ground will perhaps help us to understand some further aspects of revival in particular. For myself, I have never liked confined spaces, and to have to venture underground in the pit cage was always quite alarming, especially so in the thousand-feet-deep Lancashire mines. Having hurtled downwards at a terrific speed on a journey which seemed to have no end, the flimsy cage did eventually come to rest at that place known as *pit bottom*, a large recess, big enough to contain four, five, or even six chapel buildings. From this main station, as it were, ran narrow tunnels in all directions, into and from which shunted the coal trucks, always, always on the move, day and night. From *pit bottom* you may have had to walk very often up to three miles to get to your post, up and down the hills and dales, deep underground. I still remember how I would walk through the tunnels, thick with coal dust, hating every minute of it. Parallel with the shaft ran a pipe where, now and again, there could be heard the hiss of an air release; when this happened you would always stop for a moment's respite. It was only compressed air but, oh! it was beautiful! Deep in the bowels of the earth, where the atmosphere was usually very foul, what a relief it would be when in came this lovely, cool, compressed air! It was wonderful while it lasted, but the enjoyment of it never lasted very long, for soon the foreman would shout to us telling us to move on, and you had no choice but to obey. The beneficial effect would last for but a little longer. Very soon you would begin to droop again until you reached another air release point which you then walked past as slowly as you possibly could. So it would continue until you reached the coal face. I once worked on the *return airway* where there were no air releases. You can imagine how horrible that must have been!

But, you know—this is the point I wish to make—it remains a fact, which I can honestly declare to this day, that I would still suffer willingly, going through the whole of it all over again, in order to have the next experience—that of *going up* to the surface. It did not matter if it was pouring with rain, a thunderstorm, deep with snow, or a heat wave. When the doors opened, there we would stand grimy-faced, filthy from head to foot, stretching out our arms to greet it—oh, the real thing, beautiful and glorious and exhilarating—fresh air! As a one-time asthmatic, I cannot begin to describe how I really appreciated it, breathing in and out deeply, the fresh oxygen that we all normally take for granted.

Now then, the spiritual comparison is obvious. In the history of the Christian Church, what we see here and there are small encouragements like the little releases of compressed air in the mine. They help us along, sustain us for a while, but our aim should always be for the surface, to get up to where the air is always clean. To be in the full open air of God's grace and glory, pure and invigorating—that is revival! Why is it that we do not have more of it?

One reason is because God's people rebel. They know of the need, and they know of the testimony of those who have been in revival, but they resist. It is most strange. Although we know of His great love and even though we should be crying out to Him, we are still able to foster hard and rebellious hearts. We say something to the effect that we don't want to be made fools of or perhaps, rather, that we don't want to be exposed. We have an introverted concept of revival. We worry in case people might hear about our little sin. I sometimes fear that we would even be selfish enough to make revival tarry, if we could, so that our sin might remain hidden. We say that we do not want excitability. There is excitement in revival, yet of course, excitability on its own is not revival. We are not the slightest bit interested in the jumping up and down that is seen outside of revival. One thinks of a football match. I myself have never understood why there is such excitement about a ball being kicked here, there, and everywhere. I am far more able to comprehend and appreciate the prospect and possibility of my soul being thrilled and filled with God. I am not the type that can easily shout out *Hallelujah!* But perhaps, during a revival, God will help me to do so, not for the sake of doing it outwardly, but rather because I will be constrained to do so from the very depths of my being. It does not matter whether it is audible or in our hearts so long as it is there.

Let us consider again some of the other verses from Isaiah sixty-three:

> But they rebelled, and vexed His Holy Spirit: therefore He was turned to be their enemy, and He fought against them (verse 10).

How terrible! The tragedy of it all! How can we sin as the people of God? How can we ever contemplate doing so when we consider its consequences? Paul has surely taken from this passage the inspiration for his own exhortation and words, "Grieve not the holy Spirit of God." Furthermore, did not our blessed Saviour also say in Matthew 12:31, "Wherefore I say unto you, All manner of sin and blasphemy shall be forgiven unto men: but the blasphemy against the Holy Ghost shall not be forgiven unto men." What is this sin? We know that to reject the work of the Spirit in salvation is to reject Christ and God the Father, and that obviously means that we are lost; but it is surely much more than that. In its essence, it is rather to attribute to Satan a work which is of God: a very terrible thing to do indeed. It means, for example, that if God were to do a great and gracious and beautiful work, someone, out of spite and wickedness of heart, might then say, "This is not of God, it is of Satan." Even professing Christians can sometimes be so hard-hearted, so proud, so skeptical, and so cynical that it behooves us all to watch that our rebelliousness does not encroach into that area of sin against the Holy Spirit, thereby losing any chance of blessing.

Whole generations can pass by without experiencing revival. Many of my own friends today can testify that they have known of times when it was felt He was near. Yet somehow since those times, we have all experienced a sort of drifting away. What went wrong? Are we any the wiser now? I do not know what went wrong, but this I know: the painful cry for revival still remains. Mark well the origins of such a cry. Seek it! Nourish it! Let it begin to motivate your soul.

> Then he remembered the days of old, Moses, and his people, saying, Where is He that brought them up out of the sea with the shepherd of His flock? where is He that put His Holy Spirit within him? That led them by the right hand of Moses with His glorious arm, dividing the water before them, to make Himself an everlasting name? That led them through the deep, as an horse in the wilderness, that they should not stumble? (verses 11-13).

We have indeed sinned and have been a stiff-necked people. We have been satisfied with the run-of-the-mill evangelical norm, good as that may be, but we have not sought God. We have allowed our cities and towns and villages to become desolate and forsaken. We have hardened our hearts and become a foolish people. Yet there is another generation arising, a generation of Christians who have, for some reason, shown themselves to be very eager readers of that period of history known as the *Great Awakening of the Eighteenth Century*. In England they have re-read the story of George Whitefield and the Wesley brothers and of others. In Wales their diet has been the tales told of Williams of Pantycelyn, Daniel Rowland and Howell Harris—mighty men raised by God to change the course of history. Many men try to preach, but men raised of God are different. It is to such men that souls are drawn, are arrested, are made to listen, to believe, and to be saved.

From time to time, I have reason to visit the Cornish town of Penzance, usually to assist in preaching campaigns. On one occasion, I recall being in a book shop in that town and seeing a particular volume which I wanted to buy. It was a big book and it was expensive. For a while, because I was still uncertain about purchasing it, I kept going back to the shop, each time reading a little bit of this book which was fortunately always placed on the same shelf in the same corner. It was, in fact, the story of Methodism in Cornwall, and I wish now to recount just one incident from it. At the time of the Methodist revival there were approximately 400,000 people living in Cornwall. Of these, 10,000 were nominal Anglicans, Congregationalists, and Presbyterians. Prior to the coming of the Wesley brothers there was not much that could be said about spiritual life in Cornwall, but after their visits it is reckoned that there were 220,000 Christian men and women in the county. The Wesleys, Charles and John, would preach anywhere and everywhere, without the benefit of motor transportation. At the same time the same thing was also happening, and had been already happening for twenty years or more, in Wales. Multitudes were coming to hear Daniel Rowland at Llangeitho, not to mention other preachers at other centers. Why was this happening? Because God was on the march! Why did God allow it to happen in the eighteenth century? What is the difference between then and now? Why is it, Lord, that we are left with such dearth and desolation?

A cry is brought forth in the heart, a spiritual longing is born within; small it may be in its beginnings, but it is nevertheless a very, very important birth. I wonder whether this cry of longing and hunger for revival has been born in your own heart this day? We know, of course, that a fully developed burden for revival is a weighty thing; that is why we begin first with the cry. Can you just begin first of all to say, "Yes, maybe it is possible, Lord?" If you can, it is then also that this cry begins to take hold of your heart. It is a seeking after that which we now know can happen.

> As a beast goeth down into the valley, the Spirit of the Lord caused him to rest; so didst Thou lead Thy people, to make Thyself a glorious name (verse 14).

Why did God rescue His people in the time of Moses and in other Old Testament times? I shall tell you why: He did it for the sake of His own reputation, for the honor of His name, and for His own glory. It is not the filling of churches but, rather, the filling of a kingdom that is to the glory of God. And it is this that we desire for this generation: that Thou, O God, would see fit to glorify Thy name. Honor, Lord, Thine own name, and grant also that we might be given grace to honor Thee. Heavenly Father, grant that we might learn something about the birth of such a cry. If we began to give only the slightest hint of a cry, then He would begin to hear us. If, for example, our Lord and Saviour Jesus Christ, while being pressed by a great crowd, immediately responded and said, "Who touched me?" when that poor woman with an issue of blood was in great despair because of her illness, would He not do the same with us? Of course He would! If we truly believe that our triune God—Father, Son, and Holy Spirit—will hear the slightest little cry of "Lord, please grant revival," we will begin to be heard according to our faith. I can well imagine heaven's exclamation, "Behold, they are praying! At last, instead of just talking to one another in a prayer meeting or displaying their doctrines, they are actually praying!" They are beginning to pull—as we say in Welsh—*ar raffau'r addewidion*, which in English means literally *to pull on the ropes of the promises*, that is, to begin to draw upon the cords of grace as if they were the bells of a church tolling in heaven, ringing out the promises of God. Such praying will finally, respectfully, demand the attention of the

Almighty, leaving Him with no alternative other than to look down and grant the requests.

This is what it means to begin to cry. The cry, once it has begun, may then increase. It may become more pronounced and more importunate until it may even reach the point of anguish. It is a cry which will enable us to really lay hold upon God and bid Him:

> Look down from heaven, and behold from the habitation of Thy holiness and of Thy glory (verse 15a).

Do you notice where His habitation is? It is that place of *inheritance, incorruptible and undefiled.* There is now a growing confidence on the part of the prophet, while still retaining a reverential fear of God:

> Where is Thy zeal and Thy strength, the sounding of Thy bowels and of Thy mercies toward me? are they restrained? (verse 15b).

What joyful anticipation there is in heaven now! The prophet is beginning to cry to God. He is giving an example for us to follow. Are we still refusing to consider these things? Do we have a warmth towards those who seek revival? Lord, have we delayed too long? Has our sin been too grievous? Let me ask you some simple and yet basic questions. Do you have a quiet time at least once a day? Do you learn verses from Scripture? Do you know the truths? Do you apply them? Do you love your enemies? Do you do good to them that despitefully use you? Do you go to the prayer meeting? Do you pray there? Do you support the ministry? Do you thirst for the things of God? These are simple, little things that you can do, things that you can start off with. Begin now. After you have tackled these, you can then begin to think of greater things. The wondrous possibility is that God might eventually hear our cry and that

He might not be restrained. It fills me with dismay when I think that He might be restrained, yet without having really sought Him, I cannot know what answer He will give. But I know one thing:

> Doubtless Thou art our father, though Abraham be ignorant of us (verse 16a).

Abraham would hardly recognize us, we are so far from what we ought to be, and yet, though

> Israel acknowledge us not: Thou, O Lord, art our Father, our redeemer; Thy name is from everlasting (verse 16b).

We know we are in a mess, but we also know that we have a claim, and we are going to hold on to Thee. Although we are hardly recognizable, we know in the very depths of our being that "Thou art (still) our Father."

Can we be corrected and brought back?

> O Lord, why hast Thou made us to err from Thy ways, and hardened our heart from Thy fear? Return for Thy servants' sake, the tribes of Thine inheritance (verse 17).

Although we are seeking God's gracious help, this verse does not exempt us from our responsibility. Our God has seen fit to allow us, His people, to enter into error, not only with a view to liberal theology, but also in much of what comes under the umbrella of *evangelicalism*. The exchanges often heard go thus: "I want to do this and I want to do the other and I want to get something out of it." Then there are heard a multitude of voices competing to give us the appropriate spiritual advice: "Listen to me. Listen to that. Do this. Have you heard this? Do you want that?" Thus is the confused testimony of our evangelical faith today. I have found myself ministering to such an age, and so have many of you. We have been born for such a time as this, and we have to face up to this terrible confusion.

> The people of Thy holiness have possessed it but a little while: our adversaries have trodden down Thy sanctuary (verse 18).

Our sanctuaries are trodden down. True religion is despised. There is anguish in the hearts of God's people, but there is also, I hope, a determination. We are still Thine! Look at the next verse:

> We are Thine: Thou never barest rule over them; they were not called by Thy name (verse 19).

This picture reminds us of the story of Jehoshaphat at the time when he heard the messenger declare that the enemy was coming at him with a huge army, the time when the tramping of feet could be heard echoing from all directions, leaving Jehoshaphat trembling. They had even ventured to come across the sea. Judah, because it lay in their path, was to be annihilated. Note the account as it is given to us in 2 Chronicles 20:3-13:

> And Jehoshaphat feared, and set himself to seek the Lord, and proclaimed a fast throughout all Judah. And Judah gathered themselves together, to ask help of the Lord: even out of all the cities of Judah they came to seek the Lord. And Jehoshaphat stood in the congregation of Judah and Jerusalem, in the house of the Lord, before the new court, And said, O Lord God of our fathers, art not Thou God in heaven? and rulest not Thou over all the kingdoms of the heathen? and in

Thine hand is there not power and might, so that none is able to withstand Thee? Art not Thou our God, who didst drive out the inhabitants of this land before Thy people Israel, and gavest it to the seed of Abraham Thy friend for ever? And they dwelt therein, and have built Thee a sanctuary therein for Thy name, saying, If, when evil cometh upon us, as the sword, judgment, or pestilence, or famine, we stand before this house, and in Thy presence, (for Thy name is in this house,) and cry unto Thee in our affliction, then Thou wilt hear and help. And now, behold, the children of Ammon and Moab and Mount Seir, whom thou wouldest not let Israel invade, when they came out of the land of Egypt, but they turned from them, and destroyed them not; Behold, I say, how they reward us, to come to cast us out of Thy possession, which Thou hast given us to inherit. Oh our God, wilt Thou not judge them? for we have no might against this great company that cometh against us; neither know we what to do: but our eyes are upon Thee. And all Judah stood before the Lord, with their little ones, their wives, and their children.

What happened? In response to Jehoshaphat's prayer, God came down. We know that this is how God is moved, yet it takes us seemingly a whole age to get to this point.

We fail so often because we try to do His work for Him instead of calling upon Him. If you ring the emergency services by telephone, you call an ambulance, the police, or the fire service. Put yourself at the scene of a great fire and imagine someone saying, "I agree there is a fire, and I know that it is most unfortunate. We must rescue what we can but I do not want the fire service and police involved." There we are, hesitating, with our finger poised—"Will I, won't I?" There is a great need, multitudes are going to hell, there is a dearth in the Christian Church, and it is time to sound the alarm so that the rescue service of God might enter into the situation. Have you yourself made the emergency call, and are you listening for the bells so that you will know that the rescue service is coming? This is what it means to be crying to God and believing in God.

Again I hear you say, "It's not convenient!" Amy Carmichael of Dohnavur once had a dream where she saw millions of blind people falling over a cliff to their deaths, and also in her dream, she found herself asking the obvious question, "Is there nobody to warn them? Can they not be told, so they might not walk over the cliff?" Then suddenly, out of the corner of her eye, she saw groups of people sitting comfortably in circles, spending the whole of their time making daisy-chains! We can imagine them saying to each other, "Will we, won't we, do something? Should we, should we not, get involved?" Meanwhile the people perish! Dear Christian believers, it is no time to play at evangelicalism; now is the time to pray and to be in earnest. Is not God always a God who is in earnest? Does not God damn souls? Does not God save souls? Hell is reserved for the lost! Heaven is reserved for the found! Hell is abysmal! Heaven is glorious! Our God is always in deadly earnest. Our church, your church, is fooling around, while God is in earnest. It is high time for us, too, to be in earnest about the things of God. God is a jealous God, jealous for His own Name's sake and also for the well-being of His Church. He is both jealous and zealous for His own glory, and so should we be.

Let me close this chapter with a quotation by Jonathan Edwards describing the scene in New England in 1735:

Thus religion lay as if dying and ready to expire its last breath of life in this part of the visible church.

This was followed by a glorious contrast:

The town seemed to be full of the presence of God; it never was so full of love, nor so full of joy and yet so full of distress, as it was then. There were remarkable tokens of God's presence in almost every house. It was a time of joy in families on account of salvation being brought unto them: parents rejoicing over their children as new born, and husbands over their wives, and wives over their husbands. The goings of God were then seen in His sanctuary. God's day was a delight and His tabernacles were amiable. Our public assemblies were then beautiful. The congregation was alive in God's service, everyone earnestly intent on the public worship, every hearer eager to drink in the words of the minister as they came from his mouth. The assembly in general were, from time to time, in tears while the Word was preached; some weeping with sorrow and distress, others with joy and love; others with pity and concern for the souls of their neighbours. . . . God was in our midst.

I wonder if I will succeed in bringing a longing for such a thing as this into your heart? I will again plead with you, if you will but consider. It is something indescribable, something *par excellence,* when God visits His church with a time of His special presence. It is not a release of compressed air for a little while; rather, it is the real thing in all respects; it is the beautiful, pure, spiritual fresh air of God. "Lord look down, and remember Thy covenant of old." May He visit us, may He have mercy upon us, that we also may be able to say, "To God be the glory, great things He hath done!"

Chapter 3

THE BURDEN FOR REVIVAL
(Isaiah 64:1-7)

In our concern for the glory and honor of God, over the years we have tried nearly everything we can think of to promote success, but we must conclude that we cannot manage without God Himself. His touch alone will suffice. We have no option in this matter. Only revival will meet our need. There are certain times when individual people and ministers can be said to have received this fresh touch from God whereby they have been changed markedly. It may have happened during a meeting or through a word in season, and they have become like a new thing. A church can also undergo the same experience. We know of such times in the history of the Church when she has languished and needed such encouragement from God. Oh, that we in our time might have a touch from God and know that it is for His glory, not contrived, but a work of His sovereign grace!

So far, we have been looking at the need for revival in Isaiah sixty-two, and the cry of a man who cares for revival in Isaiah sixty-three. It is in the first seven verses of Isaiah sixty-four that we now find something of the burden for revival:

Oh that Thou wouldest rend the heavens, that Thou wouldest come down, that the mountains might flow down at Thy presence, As when the melting fire burneth, the fire causeth the waters to boil, to make Thy name known to Thine adversaries, that the nations may tremble at Thy presence! When Thou didst terrible things which we looked not for, Thou camest down, the mountains flowed down at Thy presence. For since the beginning of the world men have not heard, nor perceived by the ear, neither hath the eye seen, O God, beside Thee, what He hath prepared for him that waiteth for Him. Thou meetest him that rejoiceth and worketh righteousness, those that remember Thee in Thy ways: behold, Thou art wroth; for we have sinned: in those is continuance, and we shall be saved. But we are all as an unclean thing, and all our righteousnesses are as filthy rags; and we all do fade as a leaf; and our iniquities, like the wind, have taken us away. And there is none that calleth upon Thy name, that stirreth up himself to take hold of Thee: for Thou hast hid Thy face from us, and hast consumed us, because of our iniquities.

There is something very thrilling as we anticipate the possibility of coming revival in these words, not forgetting also something of the anguish at the consequences of our sin. I wonder how concerned we really are about having such a burden as this and also how it is that we express that concern. We can talk about the need time and time again, and sometimes even offer up a cry, but I want us to be taken on further than that, to that place where we will be unmistakably Christian in our outlook, our gaze set upon God alone and His reality, the great reality of God's own presence and beauty and power. This anonymous but very striking hymn from the Stockwell Gems collection might help to guide our thoughts to that end. It is a simple plea, addressed to God, requesting but one thing which, if granted, would satisfy all desires imaginable:

> Show me Thy face!—One transient gleam
> Of loveliness divine,
> And I shall never think or dream
> Of other love save Thine;
> All lesser light will darken quite,
> All lower glories wane;

The beautiful of earth will scarce
Seem beautiful again.

Show me Thy face!—My faith and love
Shall henceforth fixed be,
And nothing here have power to move
My soul's serenity;
My life shall seem a trance, a dream,
And all I feel and see,
Illusive, visionary—Thou
The one reality!

Show me Thy face!—I shall forget
The weary days of yore;
The fretting ghosts of vain regret
Shall haunt my soul no more;
All doubts and fears for future years
In quiet rest subside,
And nought but blest content and calm
Within my breast abide.

Show me Thy face!—The heaviest cross
Will then seem light to bear;
There will be gain in every loss,
And peace with every care;
With such light feet the years will fleet,
Life seem as brief as blest,
Till I have laid my burden down,
And entered into rest.

I am a minister in Cardiff in South Wales, and, though you might not agree, I happen to think that Cardiff is a very beautiful place. It is laid out very pleasantly with ample parks surrounding fine buildings. Although it is a comparatively small city, there are still many streets large enough to accommodate endless numbers of busy, milling people. Just outside Cardiff is Llandough Hospital, situated quite nicely on a hill. I can remember well that time when I first visited it. I had lived previously in a little village called Llanddewi Brefi, a lovely place, having a population of only four hundred fifty people, with some six or seven hundred more in the surrounding area. As you can imagine, village life held some striking contrasts when compared with Cardiff, not least the vast difference in population. I can recall driving back from Llandough into the city itself, viewing the broad expanse of the city. That which I beheld had a considerable impact upon me, more so having recently arrived from that delightful little hamlet in Cardiganshire. I did feel as if God was speaking to me, saying, "I have yet many people in this city," and I remember thinking, "Well, Lord, how will we reach them? I will never get around all these streets, should I live to be a hundred. I'll never be able to knock on every door. Lord, how will I reach all these people?" There I was, contemplating just one view out of the many aspects possible in that one small city of Cardiff alone. Had I to think, say, of London, my little mind would surely have collapsed! Then suddenly something of the great need struck me. As a servant of the Lord, a cry came into my heart which over the years has not diminished but indeed has become even more pronounced, sometimes even to the point of anguish. As I grow older and as my strength begins to fail, that anguish becomes all the more distressing, until at times it is hardly bearable.

The cry in Isaiah sixty-three leads us on in chapter sixty-four to contemplate this very kind of burden. The prophet is absolutely convinced that in the situation he describes, there is no option but to cry for God to come down. There is a natural link from verse fifteen in chapter sixty-three directly on into chapter sixty-four. That verse begins with the words "Look down"—look, Lord, take a good look—"Look down from heaven, and behold from the habitation of Thy holiness and of

Thy glory." Then he asks, as we have already noticed, "Where is Thy zeal and Thy strength, the sounding of Thy bowels and of Thy mercies towards me? are they restrained?" Thou, O God, our Father, in whom we believe, Thou who dwellest in holiness and glory, Thou who art mighty and powerful, perfect in Thine attributes, where art Thou, Lord? Look at our plight, for here we are as always in frenzied activity, and yet, Thine own presence and power, the power of Almighty God Himself, is not seen amongst us. It is Thee, Thine own self, that we lack.

> Oh that Thou wouldest rend the heavens, that Thou wouldest come down, that the mountains might flow down at Thy presence (verse 1).

Let me give an illustration, not my own, but borrowed from a sermon I heard recently. The very vivid picture which the preacher used to make his point was presented as follows. If a policeman puts his hand up to stop your car, then of course you must immediately halt your movements, not just because he is a human being but also because he is dressed in a certain uniform. You know he belongs to the police force and that he acts and directs the traffic with the backing of the Chief Constable and ultimately with the full support of the law of the land. But should the Chief Constable come along and say, "Don't take any notice of this man because, although he wears a policeman's uniform, I have stripped him of his power and authority," then presumably you would smile at the policeman, wave, and pass him by. Spiritually we are almost like that policeman. We preach, but where is the authority of God? We plead with men and they hear us with their minds, but their hearts are not moved. I am not saying that this is invariably true but that it is, sadly, all too often generally true. It is as if the prophet were on his own—left, abandoned, useless, power-less. Oh, look down—indeed, come down—so that not only may Thy authority be with me, but that Thou Thyself mayest agree to be there, standing by my side, so that the people may see and understand that the authority and glorious power of heaven itself is with me as Thy servant, aiming, winging, and making the words penetrate the very souls of men as they are preached.

What exactly is the situation in our own land today? Let me use another simple illustration. Some of you may remember the beautiful summer of 1976 in Wales. The weathermen called it a drought, but initially most ordinary people called it a glorious heat wave. The days passed and we found that gradually the plants withered and the countryside changed color as the green became a kind of reddish brown. A little later on, when water restrictions were introduced, we saw empty reservoirs revealing their submerged villages. Then we became still more concerned, and people began to say, "Well, perhaps we shouldn't worry too much. It will be alright in the end. Let's hope it rains quite soon." When the rain did not come, we then became increasingly anxious. More serious comments were heard such as, "Indeed, this is a drought of the kind we have not known before." Yet we did know that although we experienced some amount of worry, our predicament was still as nothing compared to those countries where it had not rained for five years! There is drought and there is drought!

We are, I am sure, only too familiar with those pathetic and heart-rending pictures on the television screen: images of mothers trying to feed their hungry children, children with enormous tummies and little arms like pencils; a sight that pains the heart so much that you do not want your mind to dwell too long upon it. If you do, then not only do you see the need, but your heart cries out to such an extent that this concern also soon becomes a burden. We make a contribution; we might even organize transport for water and grain to be brought to these countries. Of course this helps, yet all the while—applying the illustration—we know that the only real and lasting help is the hope of rain which comes from above.

Please don't misunderstand me. I am not belittling actual physical drought. Perish the thought! All I am doing is drawing attention to another kind of drought, a spiritual drought which is also present, not only in distant lands but on our own doorstep, even in this very day.

It is hard to imagine nowadays, but there have been times past when our villages, towns, and cities have been alive with men and women making their way to church services on Sunday. Can you recall such times? I can remember a time recently while travelling the eighty miles or so between Aberystwyth and Caernarfon, when I passed only one person going to chapel; I am sure there were more, but I passed only one! There was a time when people could be seen walking miles and miles to their places of worship, but now you would have to conclude that there is such a drought in this land that even when we have actually arrived at our chapels and church-es, it seems as if the taps have run dry, that there is no water even in the wells!

And what about the Lord's people? What about the rem-nant? You know, whereas these things should sober us, it remains a sad fact that we Christians have the same pleasures, the same enjoyments, the same holidays, the same everything as the world has. We may not sin like people in the world do, but in all else possible we go shoulder to shoulder with them. It grows worse and worse. How far will things have to go before we begin to say, "Lord, something has got to be done?" Yet, nothing is done. Some of us do things. We try this and that and the other. We try to bring little buckets of blessing. We bring in one man and then another. We say, "Have you heard of that preacher over there? He is quite a good man. He is an excellent speaker, and he is used. Let's get him to come." He comes with a couple of buckets of blessing, but what is that in a drought? What are they amongst so many? We need a drenching. We need showers of rainfall from heaven and the only one who can provide them is God. The feeble efforts of men, as earnest and as sincere as they may be, will no more suffice. We need God to look down and then to come down.

In this picture in Isaiah sixty-four, the prophet sees the great potential. He has the vision. What is it? Verse one again: "Oh that Thou wouldest." There is a plea included—a plea which if granted would result in the glorious manifestation of God's power here described. Let us also, as hearers and readers, be captivated by this wonderful potential.

> Oh that Thou wouldest rend the heavens, that Thou wouldest come down, that the mountains might flow down at Thy presence, As when the melting fire burneth, the fire causeth the waters to boil, to make Thy name known to Thine adversaries, that the nations may tremble at Thy presence! (verses 1-2).

Who is Isaiah addressing in these first two verses? Is he addressing men? No. He is addressing God! That is the vital difference. There comes a time when we are constrained to consider the Author of it all, a time when we have to recognize the Head of the Church, namely Christ Himself. The prophet is saying, "I am asking You to look. I am asking You to come—nobody else. It's You alone whom we are now seeking." He is pleading like this for God Himself to break into the situation.

Who then is he really inviting? What sort of God is He? Have you got a picture of Him in your mind? He is a God who is absolutely perfect in all His attributes. If, for example, you think first of His love, it is a love which passes knowledge. We cannot measure His love; we can only understand and experience some of it. Then again, when we think of His holiness, we catch really but a glimpse of His purity and righteousness. We should wonder rather how we can look upon Him and still live, and what that must mean when we actually do meet with Him. Our hymns very often endeavor to describe these divine attributes in a most beautiful way—Walter Chalmers Smith's famous hymn, for example:

> Immortal, invisible, God only wise,
> In light inaccessible hid from our eyes,
> Most blessed, most glorious, the Ancient of Days,
> Almighty, victorious, Thy great Name we praise.
>
> Unresting, unhasting, and silent as light,
> Nor wanting, nor wasting, Thou rulest in might;
> Thy justice like mountains high soaring above,
> Thy clouds which are fountains of goodness and love.
>
> To all life Thou givest, to both great and small;
> In all life Thou livest, the true life of all;
> We blossom and flourish as leaves on the tree,
> And wither and perish—but nought changeth Thee.
>
> Great Father of glory, pure Father of light,
> Thine angels adore Thee, all veiling their sight;
> All laud we would render; O help us to see
> 'Tis only the splendour of light hideth Thee.

How do you personally think of Him? In another hymn, it is as if the hymnist, this time Frederick William Faber, finds himself making a discovery:

> My God, how wonderful Thou art,
> Thy majesty how bright!
> How beautiful Thy mercy-seat,
> In depths of burning light!
>
> How dread are Thine eternal years,
> O everlasting Lord,

By prostrate spirits day and night
Incessantly adored!

How wonderful, how beautiful,
The sight of Thee must be,
Thine endless wisdom, boundless power,
And awful purity!

O how I fear Thee, living God,
With deepest, tenderest fears,
And worship Thee with trembling hope
And penitential tears!

Capture then a glimpse of our glorious God. Allow Him to fill your mind, your heart, and your soul with worship. God, righteous and holy, perfect in love, omnipotent, omniscient, omnipresent, infinite, eternal, and good; He is all of these unto absolute perfection. Think of Him, the God who is the end of my journey. Isaiah, considering these things, is in a sense being very bold. He is saying, "Thou who dwellest in glory and in holiness, look down on planet earth, look down!" When he ventures his next request he becomes very daring indeed: "Look down" becomes "Come down." "Come down! God of the universe, God of beyond the universe, come down and make Thyself known unto us!" In the words of Isaiah, "Oh that Thou wouldest rend the heavens." May the length of the skies be torn and God's presence flood His Church in glorious blessing and mercy! May the power of God Almighty be unleashed in this very manner!

Let us consider again verses one and two:

Oh that Thou wouldest rend the heavens, that Thou wouldest come down, that the mountains might flow down at Thy presence, As when the melting fire burneth, the fire causeth the waters to boil, to make Thy name known to Thine adversaries, that the nations may tremble at Thy presence!

The prophet, in the remainder of these two verses, begins now to think of what would actually happen if God did come down. Consider for a moment the mountains of North Wales or, if you have been abroad and seen bigger and higher ones, think of them. Suddenly, you see this mass of granite begin to shake. In North Wales a few years ago, they had earth tremors during which people rushed out into the streets. When the earth quakes and shakes, it is a terrible experience—as if the whole world is giving way under your feet. In places like Japan, earthquakes sometimes occur which kill thousands of people, and all the while, our hearts remain largely unmoved. Here, the prophet sees these mountains as if God is taking hold of them and the heat of His righteousness is melting them, causing them to flow down like a molten river. What a terrifying sight! The ultimate manifestation of power! It is the same as saying that if God should only just incline His little finger and say, "Melt!" it would be devastatingly sufficient for us to get the point—the point being that He is indeed God! And what are we? No wonder we are described as little grasshoppers, hopping about here and there with our silly, petty, little vanities! It is surprising, is it not, that we are still enabled by the mercy of God to contain in our little minds something of the knowledge of this eternal being.

But then again there are mountains, are there not?

There are, for example, mountains of materialism pervading and restricting our vision of Him. Do you think that God can ever move a man away from the idol of his heart? Think of him polishing his car. If you come between him and his car, it is like coming between a hungry dog and a bone. He will snarl at you. Come between a man and his pleasure, and he will say, "It is my right to do this, to do whatever pleases me!" Do you think the mountains of materialism can be melted? Yes, I believe it can be done. I believe in God!

Do you believe that the mountain of hard humanism that controls the media and subtly conveys its theories on the origin and meaning of life as fact, can be melted? Yes, I believe it can be done, for I believe in God! These poor little men, if they were but to experience one little tremor to shake their seemingly safe world, would straightaway be calling out, "Oh God, help me!" If their health failed or if they had a heart attack—a small tremor indeed—they would soon call out again, "Oh God, help me!" Yet their talk is so big, as if they understood the order of things. Can such humanism and such pride be melted? Yes, I believe it can be done because I believe in God!

Can all the hatred of truth, the hatred of our glorious faith in the infallible, inerrant Word of God, can that hatred ever be removed from the hearts of men and women? Can such hardened hearts, entrenched in unbelief, be transformed? Yes, I believe it can happen because I believe in God!

Then, there are of course the mountains of sin itself, mountains and mountains of pampered sin. People argue, "Well, you only live once," and with their own consent, their sin sticks to them with the tenacity of a leech. Do you think that they and their sins can be moved? Of themselves, they will not be moved, but then again, "with God all things are possible!"

Then there are mountains of what might be termed Christian unbelief. Oh yes, there is unbelief also in our own hearts. Some of us do not really believe in revival at all, let alone that God could move a city with all its vast modern estates and areas of housing developments. Think of cities like Manchester, Birmingham, London, and Liverpool. We find ourselves saying, "O Lord, there are so many people. It is such a colossal task." God presumably might well reply, "My dear little boy, you come up here and sit by My side for a moment. Tell me where you live." Then I would have to answer, "From here, Lord, I cannot even see the Earth. I cannot see the particular order of stars. I cannot see my solar system. It is now a billion, billion miles away!" He might undertake like this to show me the vastness of His creation, the multitudes of galaxies, the whole universe, the colors and dimensions of which I had never known, the sounds of which I had never heard, beauties I had never envisaged. He would say first of all, "Take a good look." Then He would say, "Now then, tell me about your problem." I could perhaps envisage myself making some sort of response. Maybe I would reply something along these lines: "There is a problem in the Church, Lord—in the Evangelical Church. We don't think You can move our hard hearts. We don't think You can move our unbelief. We have come to this conclusion over a long period of time. Can anything at all be done about our problem?" In answer God then laughs in His heaven and replies, "My dear little boy, go back and tell them that I am more than able to do even so hard a task as that which you have asked." Do we believe that He is able to do it? Do we believe in God?

The next verse brings us to consider the supernatural element:

> When Thou didst terrible things which we looked not for, Thou camest down, the mountains flowed down at Thy presence (verse 3).

In the 1904 revival, as in many others, there occurred a phenomenon known as *singing in the air*. It was heard at one time the whole way (some eighteen miles) from Aberystwyth to Llanilar and Tregaron over a period of about three-quarters of an hour: a singing when there could be no earthly possibility of anything else being responsible for it; such a singing as leaves a deep impression on anyone who happens to hear it; a sound that is above the melody-making of men; heavenly voices singing in a way unknown amongst mortals. Honest men lay claim to having experienced it and to having stayed on to listen further for a considerable time.

Take for example the story of a gentleman from Penmachno returning from the monthly meeting at Ysbyty Ifan. He and his friends believed, on leaving the meeting, that they had distinctly heard singing coming, to their minds, from the chapel building. Eventually the singing came nearer and seemed to derive its source not from the chapel at all but from a position right above them, from whence came glorious sounds such as they had never heard before. The Rev. D. Davies, a minister from the same district, noted his impression on that very same evening that it was as if a whole forest had been taken up with song! These events also took place in an earlier revival in 1818.

Another contemporary witness describes that same phenomenon in this way: "At first, it is melodious, faint and distant, yet increasing all the while until, eventually, it fills the sky like unto a great congregation praising God. Many had asked, hearing it, if there were meetings in the chapel at different or unusual times; when they heard that there had been none at that particular hour, they were struck with wonder because they had heard such harmonious voices as these singing in the air." It must have been a wonderful experience indeed, a heavenly choir taken up with an object of beauty beyond all description, singing its praises completely unaware of us, who would be but listeners on the perimeter; unforgettable, beautiful, and glorious; a celestial sound, delightful beyond imagining.

Let us cite a further instance of the supernatural element which sometimes occurs in revival. Helen Roseveare, a friend of many of us, was on one occasion staying in our house when she told me about a time when she was present during a revival in Zaire. She testified to having witnessed many instances of the supernatural in that revival. But there are two that I can recall very clearly. On one particular day, she was travelling in a Land Rover which her friend was driving when, in the distance, they saw what seemed to be a forest fire. Immediately

Helen had said, "We must hurry and help as many people as we can." So they both decided to rush over in order to reach this place, but when they got to the village the fire was actually above the village and below it were the people, praising and worshipping God. Then at another time, she was in a large, plain, barn-like structure where a service was being held. In those parts there commonly occurred a particularly fierce type of wind, in response to which, when they heard it coming, they would always hastily take the window shutters down rather than close them, to prevent them being ripped apart. During the particular service where Helen was present, somebody suddenly said that this wind was about to come, and very soon it did sound as if it had come, its rushing noise becoming louder and louder. In an orderly fashion, the people began to arrange themselves around the perimeter of the church, that being the usual procedure when this distinctly powerful wind came. Then it arrived, with all its sound but without a breath! Spontaneously men and women began to stand up and weep and confess. Some rejoiced immediately because they had actually expected that there would be a time of blessing, and they had already put their hearts right with God and so quickly and joyfully went into the blessing. Others, unprepared, yet Christian, confessed their sin; it was not so much a public confession because there were so many people doing it. Multitudes confessed, and as they confessed, they were forgiven, and as they were forgiven, so they rejoiced, until the place was full of this rejoicing in God. It is another world altogether, this dimension of the supernatural.

Let us listen to the truth expressed in verse four:

For since the beginning of the world men have not heard, nor perceived by the ear, neither hath the eye seen, O God, beside Thee, what He hath prepared for him that waiteth for Him.

We know that this verse can be taken as a lovely picture of heaven, but here, in its context, what God is saying is this: "When I come down in My glory, that which I have to give to My people, you would not be able to write it down, Isaiah, because you're not able to fathom it." Isaiah might be imagined answering, "But I have heard many wonderful and glorious things in my lifetime, individual experiences such as that time when I saw You in the temple." And God would answer, "But you have still not heard of the things which I have prepared for this occasion! That day in the temple, what you experienced was but the edge of My garment sweeping past you. You have really only just begun to see the things that I can show you. I will venture to fill your mind and soul and heart with a presence that you have only just dreamed about up until now!"

How do we attain this?

> Thou meetest him that rejoiceth and worketh righteousness, those that remember Thee in Thy ways: behold, Thou art wroth; for we have sinned: in those is continuance, and we shall be saved (verse 5).

I have looked at this verse and I have gazed upon it over and over again. I know that revival is a sovereign act of God, and if you or I have a burden at all, then it must come from God. All the glory goes to God, and yet we also know that human responsibility is not negated. On what terms will God meet His people? Please don't misunderstand me at this point; I am not for one moment suggesting that there are such things as pre-set conditions, but what I am saying is that God is a God who will meet His people according to His terms. There are special times, during normal services, when we are truly engrossed in real worship: times when it could be said that the presence of God was in the air, in the reading of the Word perhaps, or in the sermon. I used to be very worried about such times until Dr. Martyn Lloyd-Jones helped tremendously by affirming that these things were as they ought to be. I remember explaining to him that sometimes there would be a stillness in the congregation, when it seemed as though everybody had stopped breathing. The Word seemed somehow to be ripping the air, as if chunks of eternity were being thrust into time. Dr. Lloyd-Jones simply replied, "It is the Spirit." The Spirit's operation in this fashion can last a minute, or it can last an hour. These are but glimpses, but foretastes; in revival itself the difference is that the restraints are there no more. God then is really here, there, and everywhere—unmistakably, undeniably present.

I am glad, therefore, that many people today are talking about these things, despairing of the various methods that they have used in the past, at last beginning to talk about God, slowly coming to realize that only God Himself can provide the answer. I have noticed that some very unexpected people are beginning to tell me these things, people whom I would never have guessed had any interest whatsoever in God. I have heard unbelievers saying it; I am sure you have heard it also. Established cynics will even say it, "Only God can help us now; only God can save the situation." And what about the Lord's people? Abraham pleaded. Jacob argued in earnest. Isaiah here sets his sights on nothing less than Divine intervention. He has seen the need, the need has made him begin to cry, and his cry has now ultimately become a burden, a burden which cannot be dismissed or eased until God Himself meets with him to remove it.

Let us look at the man who is likely to experience this. With whom will God meet? The burdened man? Yes, but also, says verse five, "him that rejoiceth and worketh righteousness." This man is unmistakably first and foremost a Christian: his own righteousness has been taken and nailed to the cross, the penalty has been paid and the righteousness of Christ has been imputed to him by faith. This man is a man who "rejoiceth" first of all in the righteousness of Christ. Secondly, you will notice also he is a man who "worketh righteousness," which means now that he is a man who not only has imputed righteousness but also some measure of imparted righteousness. His desire in life, because he is appreciative of the salvation of his soul, is to live to the glory of God, to delight in God and walk according to His precepts. He is now one of "those that remember Thee in thy ways." He is righteous and godly. He lives by the power of the Holy Spirit and grows in grace. He is among such people that walk in a plain path, along the narrow way, without complication or contradiction. They are unmistakably Christian, taken up with the will of God. John Calvin sums up this loyalty thus:

> I greet Thee who my sure Redeemer art,
> My only trust and Saviour of my heart,
> Who pain didst undergo for my poor sake:
> I pray Thee from our hearts all cares to take.
>
> Thou art the King of mercy and of grace,
> Reigning omnipotent in every place:
> So come, O King, and our whole being sway;
> Shine on us with the light of Thy pure day.

Scripture tells us that "the effectual fervent prayer of a righteous man availeth much." Are we able to speak thus to God? Is there such a ground of appeal whereby we are able to put our case to Him regarding the dearth in our land? Perhaps some of you remember the story of Esther and the great plight of the Jews facing extinction in an alien land? Esther's burden was that she wanted to protect her fellow countrymen from this terrible end, but in those days not even a queen could approach the king without being invited. She could not just go to the king and say, "I have something to say to you. My people are going through a rough time and I am not having it!" Such an appeal would never have been permitted, and if Esther had attempted it, she would have been dealt with very swiftly indeed. Rather, because of this, she decided upon another method—she went to him, inviting him to a feast and thereby sought to exalt and honor him in his full regal splendour as king. Oh, how we have likewise forgotten how to honor God in our prayers! I can well remember, while in theological college, reading for the first time the by-now-famous quote: "God can be your friend, but you can never be pally with the Almighty." We should never, never forget that the One whom we seek to address is God. So, Esther respectfully approached her king, doing so as his queen, dressed in the right robes, just as we should be sure that we also are dressed in the righteousness of Christ. We must approach our God with reverence: "Father, Son, and Holy Spirit, hallowed be Thy name. Thou who dwellest in light and holiness, hear our petitions." Noticeably, the king did not allow Esther to present her petition until he had first seen her and was satisfied with her apparel and expression; only then did he extend his scepter, giving her permission to speak.

I believe there are similar times when we, also, can come to God knowing that He is giving us permission to ask. It is God Himself who brings us to that place; it is He who has first of all made us righteous in Christ, righteous by the grace of God. It is He, also, who has worked in us to attain some degree of actual righteousness in our lives. When we have come thus far, it is then, suddenly, that we find He is now willing to meet us. His scepter is extended towards us and He bids us make our petitions known unto Him in prayer. Samuel Chadwick once wrote, as quoted in a little China Inland Mission publication, "Satan dreads nothing but prayer. His one concern is to keep the saints from praying. He fears nothing from prayerless studies, prayerless work, prayerless religion. He laughs at our toil, mocks our wisdom, but trembles when we pray." His words have been proved only too true in so many situations.

In the subsequent history of the China Inland Mission, now called the Overseas Missionary Fellowship, the tide in many a crisis always turned when its workers met that situation with prayer and fasting. By this means many a stubborn city has yielded, many an intransigent heart has been moved, many a financial need has been supplied, and many a personal difficulty has been resolved. There is a time to ask and a way to ask.

But, let me ask you a question: does perhaps this asking involve too close a dealing for you personally? Is it too close to that place of repentance? We are, let me remind you again, dealing with, or rather, being dealt with, by God, and to me that is a wonderful thing, but it also terrifies me. Consider the sun and its heat. We all know that if the sun should come a little nearer, we would be destroyed; then on the other hand, if the sun withdrew, we would be devastated. Our God is the God of all creation. He is a God of precision and the upholder of all things. It is through Him that all things subsist. He is immense, yet He is so deft that He can put His finger forth and touch the pulsating need of my little heart. He can locate and apply, on a personal basis, amidst this enormous solar system. He can direct purposefully His grace and concern so as to reach whomever He desires on this large planet Earth, in the small land of Wales, in the little town of Cardiff, down even to the last individual mortal frame. He can put His finger on me, or He can put His finger on you. He knows how to deal with us and how to come to us without destroying us. Lord, confident in this knowledge, we are now venturing to ask again! So many years have slipped by: 1904—O thank you, Lord; 1984—O come, Lord; 1994—O Lord, have mercy; 1995—O Lord, we are desperate! How we faint and fear having to hope for the future! 1984 almost seems like yesterday, yet it is a long time ago, and the thought of waiting until 2004 or even longer breaks our hearts. Lord, Lord, pity us now! We know that we are complete in Christ. We may know something about this great need. We may feel something of it in our hearts, and yet at the same, time we know so little of the *ways* which will precipitate the rendezvous with God mentioned in verse five of Isaiah sixty-four:

> Thou meetest him that rejoiceth and worketh righteousness, those that remember Thee in Thy ways: behold, Thou art wroth; for we have sinned: in those is continuance, and we shall be saved.

"The sacrifices of God," says David in Psalm 51:17, "are a broken spirit: a broken and a contrite heart, O God, Thou wilt not despise." A broken and contrite heart! Have you ever thought what it means to have a contrite heart in an age when all the emphasis is on being H A P P Y? Why do I begrudge happiness? I do not. I am happy, I am joyous, but I am also, at the same time, consumed with grief for the spiritual state of my land and my people! I do rejoice in my Saviour, with joy unspeakable and full of glory, and yet my heart aches all the while and will continue to do so until God reveals His arm in mercy. This is why God calls men into the ministry; both the love of God and also the terror of the Lord constrains them. Then we look at ourselves generally, as ordinary Christians, and ask, "Who is going to pray?" Do we remember, or have we forgotten already, the little children of Dolgellau in 1859 who, because revival had not come to their town, met in that little room and started to recite the Lord's prayer? I can imagine us saying, "Yes, but who can begin to ask Him for such a thing today? Who among us can venture spiritually to come to such a place?" We look at ourselves and answer:

> But we are all as an unclean thing, and all our righteousnesses are as filthy rags; and we all do fade as a leaf; and our iniquities, like the wind, have taken us away (verse 6).

I am unclean, Lord, and I just do not know how to ask. You, Lord, will have to meet me. First, You will have to lift up my head and turn my face towards Thee.

Dare we imagine that things are so bad that:

> There is none that calleth upon Thy name, that stirreth up himself to take hold of Thee: for Thou hast hid Thy face from us, and hast consumed us, because of our iniquities? (verse 7).

Lord, such is our position that we cannot find a spokesman to ask for us. Our greatest fear is that You have permanently hidden Your face from us and that we may have to go on living through this continuing decline, witnessing nought but the mocking of men. Yet our cry and burden still remain. How can we be satisfied with anything less than revival?

You may be a minister in a church that holds a hundred people, thinking to yourself, "Our church is full, we are alright," or a church which holds a thousand people, thinking, "Our church is full, we are alright." Listen to yourself speaking proud, small-minded nonsense. Numbers such as these mean nothing—absolutely nothing! If we are guilty of such complacency, we should be examining our hearts in order to see how very far from God we really are. It is possible to become drunk on so very little: the activities of our own little hands and the small measure of blessing that God has given us in the past. We say we want more, but how can we really ask for more when we have been satisfied with less? We have a fear that God this time has really hidden His face from us. Is there any hope for us at all? By the grace of God, yes, there is still hope. We read of it, for example, in Exodus 33:9-13:

> And it came to pass, as Moses entered into the tabernacle, the cloudy pillar descended, and stood at the door of the tabernacle, and the Lord talked with Moses. And

all the people saw the cloudy pillar stand at the tabernacle door: and all the people rose up and worshipped, every man in his tent door. And the Lord spake unto Moses face to face, as a man speaketh unto his friend. And he turned again into the camp: but his servant Joshua, the son of Nun, a young man, departed not out of the tabernacle. And Moses said unto the Lord, See, Thou sayest unto me, Bring up this people: and Thou hast not let me know whom Thou wilt send with me. Yet Thou hast said, I know thee by name, and thou hast also found grace in My sight. Now therefore, I pray thee, if I have found grace in Thy sight, shew me now Thy way, that I may know Thee, that I may find grace in Thy sight: and consider that this nation is Thy people.

The passage serves to echo that which we have already been taught in Isaiah sixty-four, verse five: "Thou meetest him that rejoiceth and worketh righteousness, those that remember Thee in thy ways." God gives Moses His answer in Exodus 33:14:

And He said, My presence shall go with thee, and I will give thee rest.

Moses was surely glad to have been given such a promise, but consider his words yet further:

And he said unto Him, If Thy presence go not with me, carry us not up hence (verse 15).

It is absolutely hopeless if God's presence is not with us.

For wherein shall it be known here that I and Thy people have found grace in Thy sight? Is it not in that Thou goest with us? So shall we be separated, I and

Thy people, from all the people that are upon the face of the earth. And the Lord said unto Moses, I will do this thing also that thou hast spoken: for thou hast found grace in My sight, and I know thee by name. And he said, I beseech thee, shew me Thy glory (verses 16-18).

Daring, isn't he? He wants the very best that God can give him, and because he really seeks it, it is given to him. Verses nineteen to twenty-three conclude:

And He said, I will make all My goodness pass before thee, and I will proclaim the name of the Lord before thee; and will be gracious to whom I will be gracious, and will shew mercy on whom I will shew mercy. And He said, Thou canst not see My face: for there shall no man see Me, and live. And the Lord said, Behold, there is a place by Me, and thou shalt stand upon a rock: And it shall come to pass, while My glory passeth by, that I will put thee in a clift of the rock, and will cover thee with My hand while I pass by: And I will take away Mine hand, and thou shalt see My back parts: but My face shall not be seen.

Of our own selves, not one of us would be able to look fully in God's face and survive the experience, and yet there is a sense in which, through the benefits of our Mediator, we can seek His face in a spiritual manner and be granted our request. We can join in the experience of the Psalmist:

When Thou saidst, Seek ye My face; my heart said unto Thee, Thy face, Lord, will I seek. Hide not Thy face far from me; put not Thy servant away in anger: Thou hast been my help; leave me not, neither forsake me, O God of my salvation (Psalm 27:8-9).

I happen to be a father of three, and I can well remember when the children would sometimes come into a room unnoticed; then, while I would be busily talking to somebody, they would try their best always to get a little word in edgeways. They would persist and keep at it until eventually a little hand would place itself on my chin and pull me round; a little voice would then say, "Dad!" making it impossible to ignore them a minute longer.

I have an elder son, a daughter and a younger son. When I came from Llanddewi Brefi to Cardiff, I remember telling them specifically, "No bicycles! We now live in a busy city with big cars, so, no bicycles. I will make you a promise, though. When you are all seventeen, you can each go for your driving test and I will let you drive the car." That prospect seemed far enough away, and for my elder son the mere anticipation of passing his test satisfied him and, similarly, for my daughter. However, my younger son was not so easily satisfied. In the month of June, I remember him saying, "Do you know what I want for Christmas, Dad?" "No," I replied. "I want a bicycle," he answered. I ignored the request. Then he came back a little later, saying, "I don't know if you've heard me, Dad. I was talking about bicycles and I really want one." He named the shop, the kinds of bikes available, their qualities, their tires, their gears and so on. This went on for three months, until in the end I found myself telling him, "If you say that word 'bicycle' again, I will . . .!!!" I'll leave it to you to use your imagination to work out the rest of the reply I gave him. Then just half an hour later, he said, "You know the thing that I'm not supposed to talk about. . .?" I was dumbfounded—but that Christmas I took him to a shop, a beautiful bicycle shop, and bought him the nicest bicycle I could find. Why? Simply because he had been so very, very persistent. Many times I had said to him, "The other two do not have a bicycle," but he would always answer me by saying, "I know, but they are not me"—and they certainly were not!

In the context of revival also, one person may pray and say, "Well, we've prayed and nothing has happened." Another might pray and still carry on praying, saying, "I am not going to let Him go!" I am going to name it to Him in every way I can; I will make mention of "the presence of God," "the glory of God," "seeing the face of God," "the multitudes being moved," "the conviction of God," "God sweeping people into His kingdom," and "God dealing with His saints." In every way that I can, I will present it before Him and say to Him, "Look down now, O God, and come down. Rip the skies if Thou must, but cause now these mountains to flow at Thy presence." I will settle for no less!

The following hymn is also close to my heart and expresses the same desire, the same overwhelming burden for revival, which we are seeking to understand and identify with in these chapters. Oh, that Thou wouldest

> Rend the heavens, Thou Prince of Glory,
> Melt the mountains with Thy grace,
> Pour Thy presence, show Thy mercy
> And the radiance of Thy face:
> We believe that Thou art able
> In Thy greatness and Thy love;
> Make the nations fear and tremble,
> As Thou comest from above.
>
> Rend our hearts, in sorrow sighing,
> Stir our souls to seek for Thee;
> Turn Thy wrath and meet our crying;
> Help us from our sin to flee.
> There is none that seek Thee rightly,
> Yet, O Father, we are Thine;
> Come, O come, revive us quickly—
> Make our hearts to Thee incline.

Cause us now Thy way to cherish,
And Thy righteousness to hold:
Hear our plea, Lord, else we perish!
Call and bring us to Thy fold.
None have seen so dear a Saviour,
None have heard so sweet a sound,
As the name of our Redeemer,
May His praises now abound.

Thou dost meet the heart that seeks Thee,
Righteousness his robe and joy:
Thou delightest in Thy mercy
When our souls Thy grace employ.
Since the world began its journey
Eye and ear have never seen
All the wonders and the glory
God provides, beyond our dream.

Lord, the sight of our condition,
Degradation is our way:
Filthy garments our destruction,
Sin would have its evil sway;
Like a faded leaf we wither,
Caused by every wind to fly:
Brief our life and we can never
Stay the hand that bids us die.

Cause us now to call upon Thee,
Call upon the Name of names;
Stir our hearts to gaze at Calvary,
There behold reviving flames,
Holy gates of Zion City,
Now let Israel see Thy face,
For the God of might and glory
Dwells within Thy holy place.
O Lord, come!

Chapter 4

THE HOPE FOR REVIVAL
(Isaiah 64:8-12)

But now, O Lord, Thou art our Father; we are the clay,
and Thou our potter; and we all are the work of Thy
hand. Be not wroth very sore, O Lord, neither remember iniquity for ever: behold, see, we beseech Thee, we
are all Thy people. Thy holy cities are a wilderness,
Zion is a wilderness, Jerusalem a desolation. Our holy
and our beautiful house, where our fathers praised Thee,
is burned up with fire: and all our pleasant things are
laid waste. Wilt Thou refrain Thyself for these things,
O Lord? wilt Thou hold Thy peace, and afflict us very
sore?

At first glance, the concluding verse of Isaiah sixty-four seems
to suggest a rather negative end to an otherwise tremendous
chapter. The real conclusion, of course, is quite the opposite.
What we have here is what is termed a rhetorical question, the
answer to which we ourselves are left to supply. There is an
implied response: the prophet is actually rising to his climax as
he begins verse twelve—"Wilt thou refrain thyself for these
things?" The implied answer obviously being—"No!" He goes
on immediately to use the same literary device again: "Wilt
Thou hold thy peace and afflict us very sore?" The prophet
feels in the very depths of his heart that it would be inconceiv-
able that the answer could be anything but a glorious "No!"

Before we consider God's reply, let us first of all look at
the beginning of this section of Scripture in verse eight. It is as

if we are at last getting down to business: "But now, O Lord." This last chapter bears the title word *Hope*. Hope is a very wonderful thing. I am not talking about ordinary earthly hope. Those who have sat for examinations are, while awaiting their results, often asked what sort of outcome they expect. Sometimes they will answer, "Well, I hope I will be alright." They say this, of course, because they are both modest and anxious. They are not very sure how they are going to do, they just *hope* that their performance has somehow been up to standard. That is one kind of hope, the kind of hope that perhaps we are most familiar with in everyday language.

The Christian hope, however, is quite different. For example, in his first letter, chapter one verse three, the apostle Peter presents the peculiarly Christian hope as "a lively hope," pertaining to and providing us with "an inheritance incorruptible, and undefiled, and that fadeth not away, reserved in heaven." This Christian hope is, therefore, something totally different in concept and content. It is a hope that is solid, a hope that does not doubt. O that I could inspire your hearts with this particularly Christian vision of *hope*! I desire that you will finish reading this book with something of this *hope* having gained an increased sway in your hearts. More than anything else, I wish you to be fired with this burden and this *hope* as to what God can really do when He so commands it.

I recall an incident in the life of a very ordinary little lady in my own congregation. She was indeed a lovely Christian, always faithful at the means of grace in so far as she was able to be. But there came a time when she found herself failing, suffering from a terminal illness. She went into the hospital and there experienced her mind dwelling often on one particular phrase in Psalm forty-six which begins with the words: "God is our refuge and strength." When I called in each day to see her she would say, "I have been studying the Scriptures today." I would ask, "Well, what have you found to be of help today?" One afternoon her reply came, "You know that phrase, *Be still and know that I am God*? I have been on the *still* bit, and I have been still before God. He has told me to *be still*, and I have not allowed all the worries about how I will manage when I get home or whether I will be a burden and a nuisance to concern me. I have just said, 'Well, here I am, Lord. I will be *still*.'" She had learned her lesson from the Lord for that day.

Then I saw her the next day and she again said, "I have been studying the Scriptures today." I asked, "What have you seen, my dear?" She said to me, "You know, I have been looking at that word *know*—beautiful word! It was *still* yesterday, but today I am bid to *be still and know*—*know* that He is my Lord. He has flooded my soul all day with a knowledge of my salvation, of the forgiveness of my sins, of my peace with God." So she went on, "Isn't it a beautiful word? To know Him and to be known by Him."

I remember visiting her a third time, and again she said, "I have been studying the Scriptures today." "What have you been studying, my dear?" I asked. She answered, ". . .*that I am God*. Isn't that wonderful? *Be still and know that I am God.* Little me here and great God there. Isn't that a wonderful thing for me to know?" God's comforting words remained with her in this way until one day she went into a coma. Her unconsciousness was temporary, and she must have believed that she had died because after a while, when she did come round, she gave out a beautiful radiant smile! All those around her were dressed in white and she just beamed at everyone. Then the lovely smile disappeared and she said, "Oh, I am sorry. It isn't that I'm disappointed, but I thought I had gone home." That is what I would call a lively hope!

Such is the hope for heaven. But surely the Christian hope is for many other things besides? I dearly want us also to hope for great things for the Church, to have a large vision; not to have a trembling or a fearful hope, but a certain hope. I trust that many, if not all of us, are at least turning our faces towards God and that *hope* is beginning to shine in our eyes.

Where are you in all this? Have you come to see the need? Do you realize that there is a need in this country as well as in your own heart? Do you recognize that there should be a cry, that there is perhaps the tiny beginnings of one in your own soul? Have you ever considered asking God for a burden? Are you at that place where you can say, "From henceforth I will be committed." Committed to what? "Committed to the work of God." Can you say, "I want God's best for my generation, and no matter how enticing and interesting other things may be, I shall pursue God's best in this matter."

That does not mean to say that you are not vitally interested also in sanctification, godliness, and growing in grace. Of course you are; yet all the time you have this overriding concern for the glory of God in this age and generation in our land. The vast majority of people do not have the slightest idea that we meet on Sundays to worship God. If revival, however, were to really happen, there could come again times of transformation, times when the churches would be full even before we arrived! What a glorious problem that would be! Then how about thinking now in a big way? Is He not a great and immense God? The doctrine of the immensity of God is a doctrine which has been neglected and forgotten for far too long. God is a God who is very accurate and precise in knowing the numbers of the hairs on our heads and each of the sparrows that fall, but remember also that He is a God who is not limited in any way whatsoever in the scale of the work that He is able to perform. It would be but a small thing for Him to set the whole world alight with praise and worship if He but willed it so.

In Isaiah sixty-four, there is a deep concern in the prophet's heart for God's glory, the pursuit of which has become his whole life's passion. Do we not need also a similar passionate concern for the glory of Christ in His Church? I have already mentioned in the preface to this volume how books about revival very often telescope many years into their first chapters or even into that most important chapter that recounts the story of God's preparatory dealings with men and women and how, every now and again, they were given glimpses of something on the way. I still believe that something is on the way—a very wonderful something if we could only comprehend it. We must believe in the wonderful works of God in revival, and though we may not all be equally persuaded of it, it surely behooves us all to at least give our attention to these things in our generation. For my own part, I am totally convinced of its relevance, and that is why I am bringing it before you. I would, above all else, desire to see a spark kindled in your heart, flaming up into something that will influence your church and perhaps even spread out to engulf many other churches and individuals, until together we all begin to look to God for greater things than those which we now know. A work of God is always a wonderful work, and even before revival starts, men begin to glorify God in Jesus Christ, having a longing to prove His love. Charles Wesley's hymn begins to put us in that frame:

> Oh Love divine, how sweet Thou art!
> When shall I find my willing heart
> All taken up by Thee?
> I thirst, I faint, I die to prove
> The greatness of redeeming love,
> The love of Christ to me.

> Stronger His love than death or hell;
> Its riches are unsearchable;
> The first-born sons of light
> Desire in vain its depths to see;
> They cannot reach the mystery,
> The length, and breadth, and height.

God only knows the love of God;
O that it now were shed abroad
In this poor stony heart!
For love I sigh, for love I pine;
This only portion, Lord, be mine,
Be mine this better part!

O that I could forever sit
With Mary at the Master's feet!
Be this my happy choice:
My only care, delight, and bliss,
My joy, my heaven on earth, be this—
To hear the Bridegroom's voice!

These are the longings which become so very real when we move into that area of special grace in the prelude to revival, longings that Christ may be uplifted and glorified in our hearts. We may have thought that we had good and generous hearts, but then we begin to see that "God only knows the love of God; O that it now were shed abroad in this poor stony heart!" We soon discover that there is so much further to go, so much more to be had and expressed. What must it then be like to enter into that dimension of revival when He Himself descends to flood our hearts with joy unspeakable? Only then shall we be able to love in such a way that will fulfill our hearts' desire.

Ever since my youth, Psalm 133 has been used of God many times to address my soul. It is a Psalm that has come back to me at various spiritually critical times in my life. It is a Psalm that commands revival. It begins as follows:

Behold, how good and how pleasant it is for brethren to dwell together in unity!

How seemingly simple this is, along with the application which results:

For there the Lord commanded the blessing.

But, of course, it is not half so simple in practice. When we meet for our summer conference week, we find we can be united in our singing of hymns and in our conversations, especially on the fundamentals of the Faith, but supposing we remained with one another for a month? All sorts of differences would arise: doctrinal differences, personality differences, envies and even hatred. At the end of two months of each other's company, you might well find yourself saying, "Well, I don't know so much about that unity. It is harder than I thought." Unity is hard, yet God desires that there might be unity—a unity which is deeper than mere conformity whereby we believe all the correct doctrines. An agreement on the fundamentals of our Faith is a wonderful thing to have and is, indeed, a necessary basis for unity. We have a basis for unity when we are able to say that we believe in God—Father, Son and Holy Spirit—and in Jesus Christ as our Saviour; in the second coming of our blessed Lord, in the Day of Judgement, in hell and in heaven, and so on. But there is something more substantial to be had in this Psalm. Verse one again:

Behold, how good and how pleasant it is for brethren to
dwell together in unity!

When describing what a wonderful thing it is to see believers dwelling together, heart to heart, one in their purpose, with an openness of mind and affinity of spirit, he also tells us what the outcome of such unity has always been:

For there the Lord commanded the blessing, even life
for evermore.

I am sure we understand the reasoning all too well, but the big question remains: will we ever get ourselves into this blessed position? Think of your own congregation where you will often have heard or read Paul's exhortation in Ephesians 4:3 bidding the people of God to be always "endeavoring to keep the unity of the Spirit in the bond of peace." You may have said many a time, "Well, this is very good. What a lovely goal to strive for!" One day you may have found yourself praying, asking God to show you the meaning of spiritual unity because it seems to be so very important in Scripture. On the day of Pentecost, do we not read in Acts 2:1 that "they were all with one accord in one place?" They were a people who had unity! Slowly, perhaps, the significance and importance of this unity becomes more apparent to us, and we begin to ask a few more questions in prayer: "Is this something that we have to learn? And if so, Lord, teach us then what this unity is." God may well answer our prayers by showing us our own hearts, their degrees of enmity and sources of disunity. We are shocked, and we justify ourselves and say, "Ah well, there are differences. I am united enough in spirit to this person and that person and the other, but as for so and so . . . well . . ." We pause. I wonder for how long we will pause? Will it be a year? Will it be a quarter of a century, or perhaps, tragically, will we remain obstinate for a whole lifetime? Stubborn, we stubbornly balk at a simple little Psalm. We dismiss it and say, "Well, I get on with most people, I get on with them very well. You ask my friends!" But at last, God begins to deal with us, perhaps through words like this from the hymn we quoted earlier:

God only knows the love of God.

We cannot be united without this love:

O that it now were shed abroad
In this poor stony heart!

Only then do we begin to understand the meaning of spiritual unity; only then are we able to know something of what it means to be one, in heart, mind, and spirit, and delight in the things of God. If it were granted to us, it would be really as an entrance into revival.

What do we do and where do we go from here? If we examine the plea made by the prophet in the latter part of Isaiah sixty-four, we shall, I think, be guided further. Verse eight then:

> But now, O Lord, Thou art our Father; we are the clay, and Thou our potter; and we all are the work of Thy hand.

We can learn a great deal from this verse. Neither I nor any other preacher can give you revival. I wish I could come to the end of this book and say, "Now then, we'll have the revival," but that could never be. It is God's prerogative. We can only go as far as the prophet. We can only go as far as the frontiers. It is God who opens the door. It is God who opens the window of heaven. It is He, in His sovereign will, who decides when and where and what to grant in blessing.

> But now, O Lord, Thou art our Father; we are the clay, and Thou our potter; and we all are the work of Thy hand.

Have we really understood that we are nothing and can do nothing without Him? Do you think yourself to be anything? Whether you are a preacher, church officer, or a member of a church—whatever position you may have—do you really consider yourself anything or to be anybody of note? Rather, should it not be that even though we have come into that lovely area of grace where we know Jesus Christ as our Saviour and

have peace with God, we should always be very much aware of
our own unworthiness.

I remember discovering to my delight, amongst the congregation of my second church, a Welsh church at Llanddewi Brefi
in Cardiganshire, a few people who had experienced and lived
through the revival of 1904. At first I found, strangely, that I
was a little irritated by them, not in a nasty way at all, but I felt
somehow as if I wanted to correct them all the while. They
would pray, thanking God for salvation, for the forgiveness of
sins, for peace with God, and then they would say, "Lord, we
are miserable offenders. Lord, we do not please Thee, and we
do not love Thee as we ought." Having been brought up at that
time in the strict school of the Inter-Varsity Fellowship, and
knowing the doctrinal statement, Calvin's theology, and
Berkhof as well, I would find myself saying, "They have got it
wrong. Where is their assurance?" They were wise enough to
be gentle with me in their response, for they were people who
had known revival. They were people who knew that when God
draws near, even though it may be right to have confidence in
the grace of our Lord and Saviour Jesus Christ, that still does
not prevent you from trembling in His presence. Rather, a
reverential fear of God is always one of the major hallmarks
denoting an authentic visitation from above. These revival
people would sing the words of *How Great Thou Art* and mean
them! They had understood the immensity, the purity, and the
greatness of God, so that always in their assurance there was a
note of astonishment and an awareness of their unworthiness.
They were right in their view of things, and I was wrong.

Thinking still of verse eight, consider just the first statement:

But now, O Lord, Thou art our Father.

I wonder if this is true of everyone reading this book? In his
epistle to the Romans 8:15, the apostle Paul describes the man

who cries from his heart, "Abba, Father." You have really got to be in that place where you are able to cry, "Abba, Father." What does this entail? How does it come about? Paul is actually saying the word *Father* twice. First it is in Aramaic, the native tongue; for us that would correspond to English or Welsh. Then he pronounces the same word *Father* in the Greek. There is somehow a special warmth and depth in the phrase as it is expressed. What he is saying is this: "I have believed in God, I have believed in the Trinity, I have believed in my great need of God, and I have seen that it is in Christ alone that I can have the forgiveness of sins and peace with God." Not only this, but from his heart, he is also able to say, "I know that I love Thee, I know Thou art mine; and if ever I loved Thee, Lord Jesus 'tis now." Having already known and experienced all of this, there now rises this wonderful cry, "Abba, Father," to give crowning expression to all that he feels toward God. Let me ask you the question: are we beginning to get ourselves into this area spiritually? We all know that there is such a thing as a Christian going on with the Lord, that there is such a thing as pursuing God but then, there is also such a thing as having a passionate love for Christ. Such are the people who have it, that when they turn to God they are not afraid to say "We are but clay," because they know that He has had mercy upon clay.

I can remember many years ago, Pastor George Griffiths of Cwmtwrch, South Wales, praying, "Lord, we are the dust of Earth, but Hallelujah! Thou hast made sons out of dust." We are but clay. Do we admit it or do we deny it still? Can I still hear grumblings, murmurs of denial? Can I still hear you say, "No, I am special. I am a knowledgeable Christian with many experiences. I am advanced and mature." We should be very cautious of that expression, *mature Christian*. God's Word tells us that, whatever we may be, we are still clay. Do you know the lovely chorus:

Spirit of the Living God,
Fall afresh on me!
Break me, melt me,
Mould me, fill me!
Spirit of the Living God,
Fall afresh on me!?
W. G. Hathaway

Wonderful words, are they not? Our hope is eventually to come to that place where we can say, "Lord, I am clay, but I am willing, arrogant as I have been, to be broken, to have a broken and contrite heart which thou wilt not despise. Lord, I am willing to let Thee melt my hard heart." We have little hard areas we want to keep for certain enemies, but we must be able to say, "Break me, melt me. Lord, what can you make of me? Mould me! Make something of me! Make me a vessel and then Lord, do not leave me empty, but fill me with the love and the grace and the joy of God!"

In Jeremiah eighteen, using the same simile, the Bible tells us to:

Arise, and go down to the potter's house, and there I will cause thee to hear my words (verse 2).

And so the prophet Jeremiah goes on:

Then I went down to the potter's house, and, behold, he wrought a work on the wheels. And the vessel that he made of clay was marred in the hand of the potter: so he made it again another vessel, as seemed good to the potter to make it (verses 3-4).

Have you ever visited a real-life potter and seen how every now and again one of the pots is marred? What does the craftsman then do? Does he try to improve it here and there? No, he completely remakes it. Note verse four again:

> So he made it again another vessel, as seemed good to the potter to make it.

This is how we apply the lesson: although we know we are complete in Christ, we often have to cry out to the Lord, "I have not loved Thee, there is very little love in my heart, nor is my heart broken or contrite. There is need for Thee to break me down, to mould me, and to remake me that I might be a glorious vessel, fit to receive the blessing of the Lord."

> Then the word of the Lord came to me, saying, O house of Israel, cannot I do with you as this potter? saith the Lord. Behold, as the clay is in the potter's hand, so are ye in Mine hand, O house of Israel (verses 5-6).

As Christian people, we can become so very hard that we can be afraid of blessing and afraid even of God. We can be so unwilling and stubborn. Can you believe, really believe, O house of Israel, that He can make you like new? This is the possibility that is presented to us in Jeremiah.

Returning to Isaiah sixty-four, the same basic appeal continues:

> Be not wroth very sore, O Lord, neither remember iniquity for ever: behold, see, we beseech Thee, we are all Thy people (verse 9).

We can see here, very importantly, that the aim is not to run down or despise ordinary Christian believers; rather, the contrary. The prophet of course recognizes the inadequacy and iniquity yet, at the same time, he is still able to maintain that "we are all Thy people," although sometimes hardly recognizable as such. Abraham would not perhaps recognize us immediately at first glance, due to our frail hearts and small faith, and yet because of some faith, we are still "Thy people." On this basis, that we are God's people, we still have our claims upon Him, and we can still sue Him and still, therefore, "come boldly unto the throne of grace, that we may obtain mercy, and find grace to help in time of need."

In John seventeen, our Lord Jesus Christ's high priestly prayer, we can see listed the blessings that He undertakes to give to us. There, also, He prays for us, entreating His Father, reminding Him as it were of the position of all Christian believers that "they are Thine" and that "they are Mine." He further asks that His Father may see fit also to keep His own—to keep them in this world, in all the difficulties that they have, to keep them from evil and Satan and to sanctify them in His truth. Then what is in many ways the climax comes in verse twenty-two: "And the glory which Thou gavest me I have given them; that they may be one, even as We are one." What a request! Unity is prayed for. Unity is achieved already in essence, though not always, perhaps, in outward practice, yet precisely, because of this request even practical unity does now become a realistic possibility! God can now take hold of Psalm 133 and make it a living reality, all because the Man in heaven, our blessed Saviour, our Advocate on the right hand of the Majesty on High, has prayed His high priestly prayer. We are one; all of God's people are one, "even as we are one." This is the unity already established, but with the help of the Spirit, this unity can be discovered, nurtured, and secured, also, in the practical everyday life of the Church.

Next in Isaiah sixty-four, the prophet reminds God of the continuing plight of the Church, for these wonderful blessings have not yet arrived. The present reality is very different. It is both sad and tragic:

Thy holy cities are a wilderness, Zion is a wilderness, Jerusalem a desolation. Our holy and our beautiful house, where our fathers praised Thee, is burned up with fire: and all our pleasant things are laid waste (verses 10-11).

If you have ever attended a chapel that you have loved all your life and can remember a time when the building hosted a vast congregation, what a terrible experience it is to have to watch the numbers dwindling. Worse, a time may come when the bulldozers and contractor's vehicles move in, pounding down the walls. You could watch with amazement and tearful disbelief saying, "What are they doing to our beautiful place? Zion has indeed become a desolation."

An illustration comes to mind. As a student in Aberystwyth, I always chose to preach locally because it was too far to go home every weekend to Lancashire and preach in that area. I remember going to one coastal town in which was situated a lovely little chapel. One of the congregation said to me, "We are going to have a joint service tonight. The Congregational Church of about 300 members is to join us. We have about 200 members. We shall have a joint evening service because they have not got a preacher today." That evening there were only seven of us! I preached to the seven, after which an elder got up. He was from Blaenau Ffestiniog and could remember the 1904 revival, but as he recounted the memories, he turned to me and waved his hand to the mostly empty pews and said, "An enemy has done this!" He was a big, strong man and he began to weep. I had never seen an elder weep—never! Elders did not weep. I had never seen a tear shed by an elder—they were always so polished and composed—but this elder was weeping and I did not know what to do, so I simply gave the Benediction, which was about the only thing I could think of doing. I was inexperienced in such situations and was not entering into what was in that man's heart. Now perhaps I do understand. How does the Psalmist put it?

> By the rivers of Babylon, there we sat down, yea, we wept, when we remembered Zion (Psalm 137:1).

That is what this elder was doing. He was remembering Zion and he was weeping. We could apply it to ourselves. Verse three of the same Psalm reads:

> For there they that carried us away captive required of us a song . . . saying, Sing us one of the songs of Zion.

People—unbelievers—will sometimes literally ask us to do this, saying, "Come on, we hear that Welsh people sing very well!" I know that the songs of Zion are not restricted to Welsh hymns, but allow me to draw out the lesson. How do we answer the request? Should we not reply as did the Psalmist:

> How shall we sing the Lord's song in a strange land? (verse 4).

Yet, although we cannot sing, neither can we forget:

> If I forget thee, O Jerusalem, let my right hand forget her cunning (verse 5).

God sees our tears, as when Hezekiah also turned to the wall and wept. God, you may remember, responded (2 Kings 20:5), "I have heard thy prayer, I have seen thy tears." I am not saying that we should necessarily encourage emotional praying; nevertheless, there is such a thing as a weeping that comes spontaneously from burdened hearts. We can weep within or without; we can weep with our eyes or we can weep in our hearts. Oh, that we might be so burdened that God might say,

"I have heard thy prayer, I have seen thy tears." Thus, we will be beginning to pull on the cords of the heart of God.

What is revival? I have mentioned already that Dr. Sprague gave us a beautiful description in saying that it is a revival of scriptural knowledge—you will hear people weaving Scripture into their prayers for they will know their Scriptures and apply them in life; that it is also a revival of true piety, where God's people will worship Him with reverence and respect, in Spirit and in truth; that it is, lastly, a revival of practical obedience—God's people will not be backward in helping the poor and those in need. But there is yet more. This is what revival is to me: it is above all else a vision of Christ, a vision of His person such as that expressed for example in William Gadsby's hymn, a realization that

> Immortal honours rest on Jesus' head,
> My God, my portion, and my living Bread;
> In Him I live, upon Him cast my care;
> He saves from death, destruction and despair.

> He is my refuge in each deep distress,
> The Lord my strength and glorious righteousness.
> Through floods and flames He leads me safely on,
> And daily makes His sovereign goodness known.

> My every need He richly will supply,
> Nor will His mercy ever let me die;
> In Him there dwells a treasure all divine,
> And matchless grace has made that treasure mine.

> O that my soul could love and praise Him more,
> His beauties trace, His majesty adore,
> Live near His heart, upon His bosom lean,
> Obey His voice and all His will esteem.

Oh! to be immersed in the glory of Christ, with the Holy Spirit turning my gaze constantly upon my beautiful, beautiful Saviour! An understanding, rather an experience, a comprehension of His wonderful being and His inestimable saving power—is not this the meaning of revival? He is the God who shakes prisons and shakes and saves prisoners and jailers alike. Think of what this God could still do yet again! Think of Psalm 126:4, a prayer that actually asks Him to do it: "Turn again our captivity, O Lord, as the streams in the south." This is a truly remarkable thing to ask for since deserts have no streams! So it will be just as remarkable and just as miraculous when God revives His Church. It will be just as unexpected as it would be to see streams suddenly bursting forth in that vast, southern Judean desert. We need to be turned from the captivity of our apathy and indolence, from our carelessness and laxity in the things of God. What a miracle it would be to see these streams of grace, beauty, and joy spreading throughout the land!

Yet there is still an important question for us to answer—do we really want it? We read in Psalm 110:3, "Thy people shall be willing in the day of Thy power." Can you say, "Yes, Lord, I do want it." You may be a little fearful, a little bit uncertain and perhaps rightly so, saying, "But, Lord, do You think I will actually be willing for all the things that are going to come in revival? It may be that I will not like everything that happens during the revival." We may be full of hesitation, we may be clinging to besetting sins, we may be possessed with inordinate affections for various things, but nevertheless He is still willing to deal with us. God made even Jonah to be willing. We know of Jonah because of his disobedience, but God brought him back and put him where he was supposed to be.

Then there are also "the years that the locust hath eaten" (Joel 2:25). How many years have you wasted? Young people, are you wasting your best years by chasing after trivial, worldly entertainments, trying perhaps to drag all this into your Christianity and calling it holy? Be honest now, you know that it should never and can never be so. You who go by the name Christian, are you fooling around with unnecessary, worthless things? Are the locusts even now devouring precious time, the time in which you should be making great decisions in your walk with God, when you should be saying, "Take my life and let it be consecrated, Lord, to Thee?" Are you willing to be brought there? He is willing to make you willing! Those of you who are middle-aged and growing old, how many years have you wasted? There have been long periods when I have not prayed for revival as I ought, and when I look at those years, it is only too apparent in conclusion that the locusts have been at it again, eating up and destroying precious, precious opportunities. However, the wonderful thing is this: when we at last realize and recognize the problem, God is a God who can restore the years that the locusts have eaten, as if they had never been. He is a God who can compensate and reimburse past failures as well as bless the future. Are you then willing to heed this tremendously generous proposition? Are you willing to come to that place whereby He will make you willing in the day of His power? You will find no other than lasting joy in the dealings of God. His power is indeed always remarkable.

Let me illustrate again using another instance taken from the 1904 revival. Early in my ministry, as I have already mentioned, I had the great privilege of meeting some of the converts of that revival. I can remember many years ago going to a Convention held at Amman-ford in South West Wales. As I was leaving one of the meetings, I could hear a pitter-patter of footsteps coming after me and somebody, almost breathless, tapped my shoulder and said to me, "I am your uncle." He was a *Welsh uncle*! Do you know what a *Welsh uncle* is? A *Welsh uncle* can be a cousin of a cousin of a cousin! He told me that his name was Huxley. I have no recollection of our family ever using his first name, George. He was always known as Huxley. My mother had told me a little about him. Uncle Huxley had gone out to the mission field when my mother was a little child of three or four years of age. She remembered also that when he was home he used to take her on his knee and sing to her the songs of Lushai in India.

That time in Amman-ford, I was so pleased to have met a saved member of the family—wonderful!—that I invited him to come home with me. He was glad because he had nowhere to go. He was a saintly man, as all who knew him would testify. He recounted to me his story. As far back as anybody could remember, Huxley had been above reproach. Huxley was a good boy. Huxley was a tidy boy. He never missed the morning Service, Sunday School, evening Service, Prayer Meeting or the Seiat, and indeed he was considered early on by the minister as a candidate for the ministry. Huxley was virtuous in every respect. Then God came and shook Bethany, Amman-ford. The meetings crowded the chapel out; people sat anywhere and everywhere. Huxley went home one night astounded, having seen men and women who were once careless about the things of God and indifferent about the prayer meeting, now rejoicing and singing the praises of Zion. Huxley's reaction was to ask the question, "What is wrong with them?" You remember, Huxley was such a good boy. "Huxley," they said, "you too need to be saved." "What?" he replied, "I am a good boy." "Go back, go back to the meeting, Huxley," they continued. It was about eleven o'clock in the evening but he went. The place was full, and as he entered, there was a Presence there that he had never known before. The power of this Presence began to churn his sinful heart. God entered his mind and his being in a way that he had never previously known or imagined possible. God was calling Uncle Huxley to repent and believe. "I heard the voice of Jesus say, 'Come unto me. . . .'" The next thing he knew, he was being carried over the heads of the people until he was in the Big Seat, sitting next to the minister, crying for the mercy of God. Such is His power.

Do you perhaps think that all this was but a passing experience? Uncle Huxley was on the mission field for fifty years. Their first little girl died in Lushai, India, in 1916. She would not have died, humanly speaking, if there had been any kind of medical attention. A son was born but he also suffered an illness which left his mind impaired. Uncle Huxley looked after this son all his life. While staying with us he told of the greatest tragedy of all. He recalled how, after they had returned home from India, "We had just moved into our first home, which had only two rooms. My wife had always said that she would love to have a garden, and in this new home there was a garden. She was such a long time in the garden, that I decided to go out to see what she was doing. Out in the garden I found her; she had gone home to be with the Lord." At first Uncle Huxley was struck down with the thought, "God has taken her home and has left me with a son who does not really know his father. The difficulties I will have to face will be insurmountable. Then I remembered that the Lord never makes mistakes."

Huxley died when he was ninety-six; he preached until two months before his death. A flash-in-the-pan experience? Don't you believe it! The phenomenon which had taken hold on Uncle Huxley was no passing phase, rather it was the power of God from on high applying the glorious gospel of Jesus Christ unto the salvation of his soul! Such power as this, when manifested, transforms, purifies, preserves, sustains, until we are in the end taken to glory. This is the testimony to the blessings conferred by revival in the life and death of Uncle Huxley.

The mighty, irresistible power of God in the salvation of souls during revival is a most awesome thing to contemplate. The following quotation is taken from a diary written by an unlettered farmer named Nathan Cole, part of which is recorded

in the biography of George Whitfield by Arnold Dallimore.[1]
The scene is New England, 1740:

> Now it pleased God to send Mr. Whitefield into this
> land; and my hearing of his preaching at Philadelphia,
> like one of the old apostles, and many thousands
> flocking to hear him preach the gospel, and great
> numbers being converted to Christ, I felt the Spirit of
> God drawing me by conviction: I longed to see and hear
> him and wished he could come this way. I heard he was
> come to New York and the Jerseys and great multitudes
> flocking after him under great concern for their souls
> which brought on my concern more and more, hoping
> soon to see him; but next I heard that he was at Long
> Island, then at Boston, and next at Northampton. Then
> on a sudden in the morning about eight or nine of the
> clock there came a messenger and said Mr. Whitefield
> preached at Hartford and Wetherfield yesterday and is
> to preach at Middletown this morning at ten of the
> clock.
>
> I was in my field at work. I dropped my tool that I
> had in my hand and ran home to my wife, telling her to
> make ready quickly to go and hear Mr. Whitefield
> preach at Middletown, then ran to my pasture for my
> horse with all my might, fearing that I should be too
> late. Having my horse, I with my wife soon mounted
> the horse and went forward as fast as I thought the
> horse could bear, and when my horse got much out of
> breath, I would get down and put my wife on the saddle
> and bid her ride as fast as she could and not stop or
> slack for me except I bade her, and so I would run until
> I was much out of breath and then mount my horse

---

[1]Volume one, page 541ff.

again, and so I did several times to favour my horse. We improved every moment to get along as if we were fleeing for our lives, all the while fearing we should be too late to hear the sermon, for we had twelve miles to ride double in little more than an hour and we went round by the upper way. And when we came within about half a mile or a mile of the road that comes down to Hartford, on high land I saw before me a cloud of fog arising. I first thought it came from the great river, but as I came nearer the road I heard a noise of horses' feet coming down the road, and this cloud was a cloud of dust made by the horses' feet. It arose some rods into the air over the tops of the hills and trees; and when I came within about twenty rods of the road, I could see men and horses slipping along in the cloud like shadows, and as I drew nearer it seemed like a steady stream of horses and their riders, scarcely a horse more than his length behind another, all of a lather and foam with sweat, their breath rolling out of their nostrils every jump. Every horse seemed to go with all his might to carry his rider to hear news from heaven for the saving of souls. It made me tremble to see the sight, how the world was in a struggle. I found a vacancy between two horses to slip in mine, and my wife said, "Our clothes will be all spoiled, see how they look," for they were so covered with dust that they looked almost all of a colour, coats, hats, shirts and horse.

We went down in the stream but heard no man speak a word all the way for three miles but everyone pressing forward in great haste; and when we got to Middletown old meeting house, there was a great multitude, it was said to be three or four thousand people, assembled together. We dismounted and shook off our dust, and the ministers were then coming to the meeting house. I turned and looked towards the great river and saw the ferryboats running swift backward and forward bringing over loads of people, and the oars rowed nimble and quick. Everything, men, horses and boats seemed to be struggling for life. The land and banks over the river looked black with people and horses; all along the twelve miles I saw no man at work in his field, but all seemed to be gone. When I saw Mr. Whitefield come upon the scaffold, he looked almost angelical, a young, slim, slender youth, before some thousands of people with a bold undaunted countenance. And my hearing how God was with him everywhere as he came along it solemnized my mind and put me into a trembling fear before he began to preach; for he looked as if he was clothed with authority from the Great God, and a sweet solemnity sat upon his brow, and my hearing him preach gave me a heart wound. By God's blessing, my old foundation was broken up and I saw that my righteousness would not save me, but the righteousness of Christ, and I became a Christian.

Isn't this a beautiful account? Can we imagine such times as these occurring again? Can you think of it happening in this wasted, desolate land that is ours? Can it ever be? Well, the answer is in this sixty-forth chapter of Isaiah. If we ask Him, "Lord, are You going to forget us in this decade?" the implied general answer is, "No!" "Are You going to be vexed forever with us?" Broadly speaking, the answer again, by implication, is "No!" But the important question now is how we see our responsibility in all of this. How do we face up to the challenge presented to us? Do we submit to the requests and act upon the entreaties that God has given to us in His Word?

> Come, let us to the Lord our God
> With contrite hearts return;

Our God is gracious, nor will leave
The desolate to mourn.

His voice commands the tempest forth,
And stills the stormy wave;
And though His arm be strong to smite,
'Tis also strong to save.

Long hath the night of sorrow reigned;
The dawn shall bring us light;
God shall appear, and we shall rise
With gladness in His sight.
Scottish Paraphrases

Let me give you one more illustration before we conclude. I was a schoolmaster for some years before I became a minister and was, at one time, form master to a class of twelve and thirteen year olds. In that class there was one greatly disadvantaged boy who did not get much encouragement at home. He was very dirty looking and untidy, and he must have had a very unhappy childhood, because every time you passed him, he used to raise his arm across his forehead to protect himself. He was a pitiful little boy and was quite a nuisance in the classroom. Yet I felt sorry for him. In my subject, art, there was a lot of cleaning up to be done after the lesson, and in those days children liked to help! They used to plead with me, saying, "Sir! Sir! Sir!" You may remember such times yourself. Then one day there came a little voice, "Sir, you never picks me." I realized immediately what I had done, or rather, what I had failed to do. The fact is you always notice the bright eyes, the clean children, the pleasant personalities, or the ones gifted in your particular subject. This little boy, on the other hand was hopeless. "Sir, you never picks me." And yet, do you know, I did love him. In a way I loved him more than any of them.

How then shall we as a similarly hopeless people approach God? The little boy gives us some encouragement, doesn't he? He gives us hope, for will not God pity us in a similar fashion. "If ye then, being evil, know how to give good gifts unto your children: how much more shall your heavenly Father give the Holy Spirit to them that ask Him?" (Luke 11:13). Will we not ask? Will we not approach Him?

"Will the gates of hell prevail, Lord, and prevent us?"

"No, they shall not prevail against the Church of God. They shall not bar the way of approach."

"Wilt Thou then forsake us, Lord?"

"No, it is written, 'I will never leave thee, nor forsake thee.'"

"Wilt Thou then be angry forever?"

"No, I will not be angry forever."

Like that little boy, we are pleading, "Sir, in our generation, we have not been picked!" God might just then say to His congregation in heaven, "I believe the saints are knocking at my window. Open it to them! Have they been undergirded and strengthened in the inner man? Are they prepared for what I have for them? Bring a vessel, bring a vessel of blessing and of grace and of joy and of power; bring a vessel and prepare now that this window should be opened, and we will pour a blessing on this people." Alternatively, He could say, "No, rather I will go down Myself!" That would be even better! That is what we want: God in the midst of us, mighty to save! How can we say this? How can we presume that He might even come Himself? It is because we know that He loves us with the same quality and measure of love that matches His love for His own dear Son. We belong to God, and so when we call in this way, we know that He will indeed come.

Gentle Jesus, when on others Thou art smiling, do not, do not pass us by!